HOW TO MAKE YOUR OWN CANE FURNITURE

HOW TO MAKE YOUR OWN CANE FURNITURE

Max and Charlotte Alth

STOBART & SON LTD
LONDON

To Misch,
Mike,
Syme,
Arrabella,
Mendle, and all other rattan buffs.

First published in the United Kingdom 1982 by Stobart & Son Ltd 67–73 Worship Street London EC2A 2EL

Published in America as *Rattan Furniture — A Home Craftsman's Guide*

Copyright © 1979 Max and Charlotte Alth

ISBN 0 85442 021 5

Printed in Great Britain by The Bowering Press, Plymouth & London

CONTENTS

Preface *vii*

Part One **Construction and Design Basics**

1
Materials   *3*

2
Tools and Equipment   *15*

3
Cutting and Bending   *19*

4
Joints   *29*

5
Ornamentation   *47*

6
Finishing and Care   *60*

7
Designing Rattan Furniture   *64*

8
Construction Tips   *72*

Part Two **Rattan Construction Projects**

9
Coffee Table (Design One)   *81*

10
Coffee Table (Design Two)   *87*

11
Clothes Tree   *97*

12
Bed Bench   *105*

13
Étagère   *119*

14
Chaise Longue   *132*

15
Tea Cart   *143*

16
Love Seat   *153*

17
Dining Room Chairs   *166*

18
Night Table   *180*

Part Three   Repairs

19
Repairing Rattan and Wicker Pieces   *193*

Appendix: Sources of Supply   *207*

Index   *211*

PREFACE

If you are old enough and fortunate enough, you may remember the peace and quiet of the sun parlors or sun porches of yesteryear, before television or even before radio.

Those were times when we demanded far less of life than we do today. Then it was more than enough just to sit and be, watching the sunlight drift in through the slits in the bamboo shades and draw shadow pictures as it passed through the wickerwork furniture and fell upon the woven straw mats covering the floor.

The only sounds were those of the birds and insects outside, the creak of the furniture as someone moved. Our entire world was there, all around us: solid, palpable in light and shade.

It is doubtful if we will ever return to that period individually or collectively; that past period when it wasn't a near sin to stop striving for an afternoon and merely sit and simply exist.

But we can re-create the period physically, and if you wish to do so but do not care to pay the exorbitant prices for designer pieces of rattan furniture, this book will help you. This book will help you design and build rattan furniture of all kinds yourself. In addition, this book will guide you to the repair and rebuilding of rattan and wicker furniture that you may have on hand or can secure from junk shops and flea markets and garage sales.

In the trade, wicker is used to describe furniture, baskets, and the like, made by weaving any of more than a dozen natural materials. Rattan, which is sometimes also woven in the process of making furniture and which is also a natural material, is never classified as wicker. It is always rattan. Often people confuse it with bamboo.

Whereas rattan furniture is easy to make, wicker furniture is not. Therefore, the making of wicker furniture is omitted.

The authors hereby acknowledge their appreciation and gratitude for all the encouragement and technical assistance given them by Mr. Sumner S. Bryant, Jr., one of this country's foremost experts on the subject of rattan.

PUBLISHER'S NOTE

This book is published in America under the title *Rattan Furniture — A Home Craftsman's Guide*.

The supply sources have been changed for obvious reasons, and the title changed because it is felt that 'Cane Furniture' is a more familiar and understood term in the U.K. for this type of furniture. It is a change of terminology only and as such does not alter the material or the techniques of using it. The text of both American and British editions is the same.

Part One

Construction and Design Basics

1
MATERIALS

Rattan furniture is constructed mainly from rattan — in most instances only from rattan and its components. In some cases portions of other plants may be used.

Wicker furniture is constructed from any of a dozen commercially used "wickers," the choice of which is not only dependent on what is to be constructed but on what is available and its cost. Thus you will find wicker furniture made from willow, reed, split bamboo, splint, and other materials, including artificial wicker made of Kraft paper.

RATTAN　　　Rattan is the trunk of any of more than 150 known species of climbing palms after the bark and thorns have been removed. These palms grow in the steaming jungles and hot-soup swamps of Borneo, Sumatra, Malaysia, and the Philippines.

The climbing palm has fronds much like your ordinary, everyday palm tree, but there the likeness ceases. The climbing palm has nasty, down-pointing thorns and is long and thin, like a vine. At its root, no known species has a trunk more than 4 or 5 inches in diameter, and these trees are believed to be several hundred years old. Generally, the climbing palm is only 2 inches thick or less at its base when it is harvested, and it may be up to 600 feet in length. Some species do not climb but grow straight up like skinny flag poles. Others may be less than ½ inch in diameter for most of their hundreds of feet of length.

In harvesting, the thin trunk of the climbing palm is cut through some 3 feet above the ground. It is then left in place for several days in order to loosen its bark and nasty thorns. The root of the plant is left in the earth. It will put forth another vine, which will be ready for harvest in another 6 or 7 years, when the rattan farmers will return.

The inside of the climbing palm is one long, almost continuous bundle of parallel fibers. The outside of the climbing palm, after its bark and thorns have been removed, is very hard and shiny. The shiny layer is actually silicon, the stuff sand and glass are made of. To some extent, the cleaned and cured rattan looks like bamboo. But whereas bamboo has a bulge where the leaf once was, rattan has a sort of rough-edged step. Very often the edge of the step is dark.

The climbing palm is very strong. In the Far East it is used for ropes, cables from which suspension bridges are hung, nets, and the like. The word *rattan* comes from the Malayan word for "walking stick" or "walking cane," *rotan*. (But some say it means "to peel off.")

Nomenclature

As stated, rattan is the cleaned, vinelike trunk of the climbing palm tree. In the trade, however, it is more often called a cane or pole.

Species and quality

No more than a dozen or so of the more than 150 known species of rattan are used for furniture making and similar applications. These are generally tagged with the name of the area in which they have grown. Best known, perhaps, are Pakkie, Oemoeloe, Kooboo, and Loontie.

Fully grown, these species vary in diameter from ⅛ inch to about 1½ inches. Larger diameter vines are comparatively rare.

So far as you and I and the native furniture makers of the Far East are concerned, one species is pretty much like another. The difference between species is mainly in ease of bending and memory (holding a bend), and this difference is of importance mainly to manufacturers using semiautomatic equipment. We bend by eye and can adjust our bending as we go. When you feed rattan or anything else to a machine, all the pieces of rattan must be nearly identical if the results are to be nearly identical.

Commercially, rattan is graded by appearance. The best grade of rattan is perfectly clean, with very little change in color and very smooth joints. But perfect rattan looks something like plastic pipe, and many people therefore do not like its appearance. Some people even confuse top-grade rattan with bamboo. In any case, unless you purchase a large quantity of rattan and pay a premium for what amounts to selection, the rattan you purchase will look like rattan. It will have growth and joint marks, slash marks, and color differences from pole to pole and even along the length of the same pole.

Dimensions

Rattan poles are available in diameters ranging from ⅜ inch on up to 1½ inches and on occasion, even greater diameters. The poles are usually cut into lengths of 8 to 10 feet and shipped to this country in bundles of fifteen to twenty-five or more poles, depending on their diameter.

Since a rattan pole is thinner at one end than its other end—you can actually measure this—and since poles are a bit thicker at the joints, where the leaves once grew, and since some poles are a bit thicker or thinner along their middles than either of their ends, it is almost impossible to order poles of the exact diameter you may wish—at least not exact in the sense the word is used by a cabinetmaker or a machinist. Very often poles will be ordered within a range, as for example, between ¾ and 1 inch. Still, within a bundle of twenty-five poles, there will be some that may measure more and less than the diameters specified. In any case, a slight variation in pole diameter is of little importance in the making of rattan furniture.

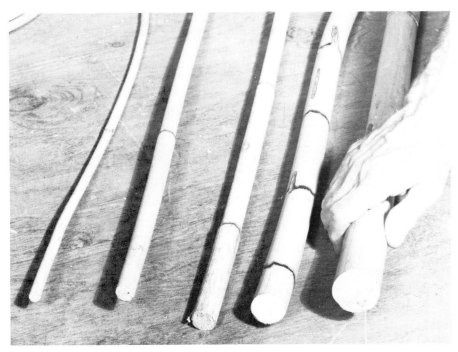

Rattan is harvested and shipped in diameters ranging from as little as ⅜ inch to more than 1 inch. Notice how the markings differ from one pole to the next and that none of the poles is perfectly straight.

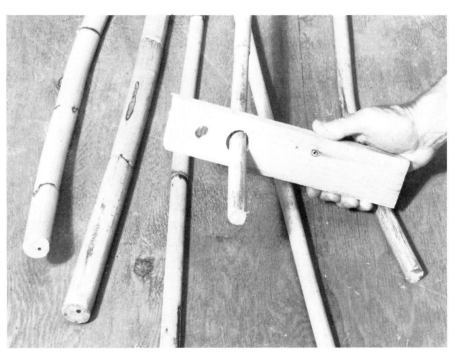

You will find a diameter gauge very handy in locating the pole you want. It is also useful in determining quickly the thicker end of a long pole. A piece of board with a couple of holes is turned into a useful tool.

A 250-foot hank of wide binding cane. No single strip is much more than 20 feet long. Some pieces may be shorter.

STRAND CANE After the rattan vines have been cut and pulled down from the trees, they are cut again into lengths of 16 to 20 feet and bound into convenient bundles. The bundles are then shipped downriver to native warehouses, where the vines are treated with sulfur to destroy insects and fungi, separated for quality and size and then soaked in water to soften the outer layer or skin of the vine. (The bark and thorns are already removed.)

Next, the surface of the vine is removed in strips about $\frac{1}{16}$ inch thick by hand or by machine. The removed strip of bark or skin is called cane, or, more specifically, strand cane because it is a strand. Each strand carries the coloration and markings of the cane from which it was taken on one side and is fairly smooth and evenly colored on the other side. Each strand is as long as the cane from which it was taken. The final step consists of recutting each strand to make its width and thickness uniform.

Strand cane is very flexible when dry and even more so when soaked in water for a short time. It is also very strong and easily capable of withstanding a pull of several hundred pounds.

Dimensions Normally, cane is cut into seven different widths from 1¾ mm, called Superfine, to 6 to 6½ mm, called Wide Binding. Generally, cane is sold in 250-foot coils and 1,000-foot hanks. One coil is usually sufficient to cane an average chair.

Superfine		1¾ mm
Fine–Fine		2 mm
Fine		2½ mm
Narrow–Medium		2¾ mm
Medium		3 mm
Common		3½ mm
Narrow Binding		4–4½ mm
Wide Binding		6–6½ mm

Actual size, strand cane dimensions. Sold in 1,000-foot hanks and 250-foot coils.

CANE WEBBING

When strand cane is used to weave a chair bottom or back, a considerable amount of time and labor is required. To reduce the time and effort necessary without reducing quality, strand cane is machine woven into a coarse fabric called cane webbing. In place it looks and wears exactly like hand-woven caning — sometimes better, because the machine-woven caning has no weaving errors and all the spaces are perfectly alike.

But note that in order to use cane webbing on a chair seat or back, the chair must be prepared for a spline (see page 00). This means that a groove must exist or must be cut to circumscribe the area to be covered. The cane webbing is placed in position over the opening and over the groove. The webbing is then locked into place by driving a spline — a long wedge — down on top of the webbing so that is is forced into the groove.

Dimensions

Cane webbing is manufactured in a variety of patterns and in widths from 12 to 36 inches, depending on the weave. It is sold by the foot, and in 10- and 25-foot rolls.

Cane webbing

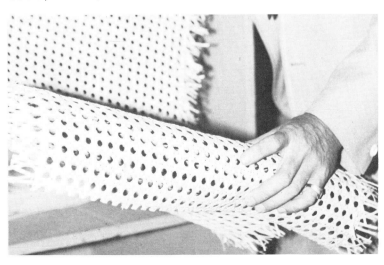

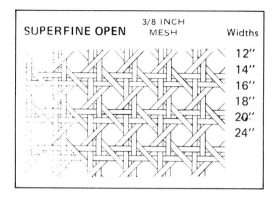

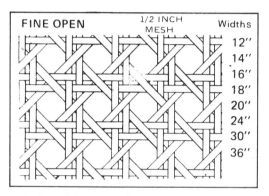

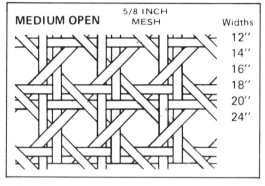

Just a few of the many different styles of cane webbing available. Courtesy, Peerless Rattan.

SKINNED RATTAN (sometimes called scraped rattan)

When the hard, shiny surface is removed from rattan, the remainder is called skinned rattan. It differs from the original harvested and cleaned vine in that its surface is no longer round and shiny, but a dull tan and composed of a number of flat, parallel surfaces left by the skinning knives.

Skinned rattan is not soil- and moisture-repellent. It is highly absorbent. To make it somewhat soil- and moisture-repellent, you must coat it with varnish or a similar material.

On the plus side, skinned rattan is bent into shape much more easily than the nonskinned rattan, and since the removed cane has value, skinned rattan costs less than nonskinned rattan. It is therefore often used for furniture parts that will be out of sight when the furniture is completed and in use. For example, skinned rattan is used for parts of the frames of wicker furniture. The wicker hides the rough surface of the skinned rattan. Skinned rattan is also used for the legs of tables and the likes that will be wrapped (covered) with cane. The cane hides the skinned rattan.

Smoothly skinned rattan

If you visit furniture shops in your search for design ideas, you may encounter a·very unusual type of rattan furniture. The rattan is smooth, with just a slight change in dimension to indicate the joint. The curves are even and identical. The rattan is shiny with many coats of varnish. At a distance the furniture may appear to be made of plastic pipe.

This is smoothly skinned rattan. The outer cane layer has been removed and the rough surface has been carefully sanded down to the core of the rattan until it is very smooth and has no marks at all.

There is nothing wrong with this furniture, except that is not rattan furniture — it is thick-reed furniture. The difference is that the hard, protective outer surface of the palm tree is gone. When the varnish wears off, as it will at the arm rests and similar places, the soft, easily stained and soiled reed is exposed. If you are careful to keep the varnish intact, or replace it as needed, thick-reed furniture will last as long as standard rattan furniture.

REED   When the last vestiges of bark or skin have been removed from the skinned rattan, the wood or central core that remains is called reed. Reed is highly absorbent, and easily bent when water-soaked.

Dimensions   The central core of the rattan, the reed, is easily shaped lengthwise. Each shape and some of the size groups are given names. Handicraft reeds have a circular cross section and range from 1¼ mm to 4½ mm in diameter. Oval reeds have an oval cross section and range from ³⁄₁₆ inch to ⅜ inch. Flat reeds range from ¼ to ⅝ inch in width. Spline reeds are roughly triangular in cross section and range from ⅛ inch in height to ⅜ inch in height. Large-size reed has a circular cross section like handicraft reed and ranges in diameter from ⅜ inch to 1¼ inches. Whereas the other types are sold by the pound and rolled into long coils, large-size reed is sold by the piece, with each piece generally no more than 5 feet long.

Note that all suppliers do not handle all sizes of reed, nor even list them in their catalogs. To find all the reeds available, you will have to consult more than one supplier.

A small coil of handicraft reed.

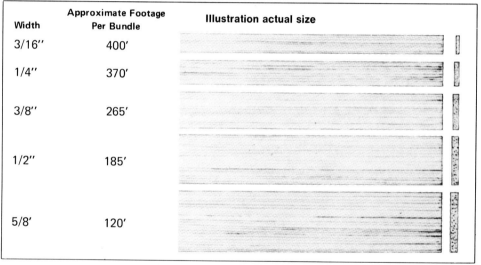

Size Number	Diam.	MM Size	Approx. Footage Per Lb. Coil	Illustration actual size	Size Number
0	3/64	1¼	2200 ft.		0
1	1/16	1½	1600 ft.		1
2	–	1¾	1100 ft.		2
2½	5/64	2	900 ft.		2½
3	3/32	2¼	750 ft.		3
3½	–	2½	600 ft.		3½
4	7/64	2¾	500 ft.		4
4½	1/8	3	400 ft.		4½
5	9/64	3¼	350 ft.		5
5½	5/32	3½	325 ft.		5½
6	11/64	4	200 ft.		6
6½	3/16	4½	160 ft.		6½

Actual size, handicraft reed dimensions. Handicraft reed is usually sold only by the coil, which usually weighs about 1 pound. Courtesy, Cane & Basket Supply Co.

Width	Approximate Footage Per Bundle	Illustration actual size
3/16″	400′	
1/4″	370′	
3/8″	265′	
1/2″	185′	
5/8′	120′	

Actual size, flat reed dimensions. Flat reed is usually sold in 1-pound bundles.
Courtesy, Cane & Basket Supply Co.

Width	Approximate Footage per Bundle	Illustration actual size
3/16″	275′	
1/4″	275′	
3/8″	175′	

Actual size, flat/oval reed dimensions. Flat/oval reed is usually sold in 1-pound bundles.
Courtesy, Cane & Basket Supply Co.

SPLINE CHART

This wedge-shaped reed spline is used to secure the woven cane to chair frames having a groove. It is very important to select the proper size spline. For example, if the groove in your chair frame is ¼" wide you would order size number 9½ as shown on chart below.

Number	M/M Size	Fraction	Actual Groove Size	Illustration Actual Size
6½	2¼ x 3¾	3/32"	1/8"	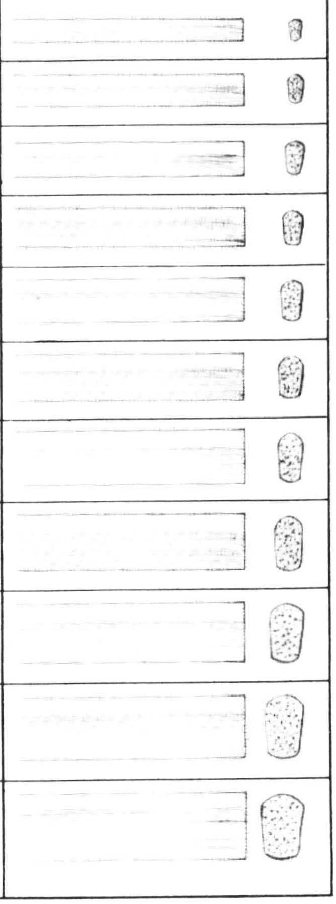
7	3 x 5	7/64"	5/32"	
7½	3½ x 5½	9/64"	11/64"	
8	4 x 5½	5/32"	3/16"	
8½	4¼ x 6	11/64"	13/64"	
9	4¾ x 6¼	3/16"	7/32"	
9½	5¼ x 7	7/32"	1/4"	
10	5¾ x 7½	15/64"	9/32"	
10½	6¼ x 8	1/4"	19/64"	
11	6¾ x 8¾	17/64"	11/32"	
12	7½ x 9½	19/64"	3/8"	

Spline is usually sold in 50-foot bundles, one size spline to a bundle.
Courtesy, Cane & Basket Supply Co.

Size Number	Diam.	M/M Size	Approx. Ft. Per Lb. Coil	Illustration actual size
7	13/64"	5	150 ft.	
7½	7/32"	5½	120 ft.	
8	—	5¾	110 ft.	
8½	15/64"	6	105 ft.	
9	1/4"	6½	100 ft.	
9½	9/32"	7	90 ft.	
10	19/64"	7½	80 ft.	
11	11/32"	8½	40 ft.	
12	3/8"	9½	35 ft.	
13	13/32"	10	25 ft.	
14	7/16"	11	20 ft.	
15	1/2"	12½	15 ft.	
16	9/16"	14	14 ft.	
17	5/8"	15¾	12 ft.	

Actual size, round bulk reed dimensions.
Bulk reed is usually sold by the foot or pound.
Courtesy, Cane & Basket Supply Co.

SPLINT   Technically — or had we best say historically — a splint was a thin, flat strip of hardwood roughly ⅟₆₄ inch thick, up to 1 inch wide, and several yards long. It was made by craftsmen in rural areas by running a wood plane down the edge of a long board. Woods such as hickory, ash, and oak were used, and are still used. Today, wood splint is made by machine.

But today the term splint has been broadened by usage to include splint made from reed. Sometimes reed splint is listed in craft supply catalogs as reed splint and sometimes merely as flat reed.

Both types are used for the same purpose, namely making the woven portion of furniture, baskets, and the like. Both types are soaked before using to make them more pliable. The differences between the two materials are not great, but they exist and are worth mentioning.

Wood splint is stiffer and a little more difficult to work with than reed. Wood splint is harder, less absorbent, and longer lasting than reed. Both will take stain and varnish equally well, and while they look alike in place from a distance, you cannot possibly use one in place of the other without the exchange being noticeable and generally unacceptable. In other words, don't use reed to patch wood or vice versa.

Width	Approx. Footage Per Coil	Illustration actual size
5/8″	45′	
1″	45′	

Actual size, ash splint dimensions.
Each coil contains six strands of splint. Each splint strand is 6 to 8 feet long.
Courtesy, Cane & Basket Supply Co.

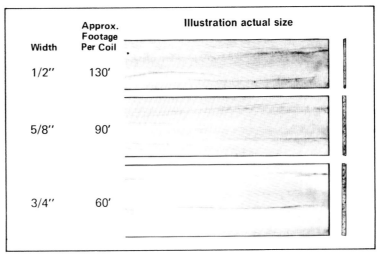

Width	Approx. Footage Per Coil	Illustration actual size
1/2″	130′	
5/8″	90′	
3/4″	60′	

Actual size, fiber (reed) splint dimensions.
Courtesy, Cane & Basket Supply Co.

Dimensions

Hardwood splint is usually available in two widths: ⅝ and 1 inch. Generally, splints, sometimes called strands, are packed six strands to a coil and are sold by the coil only. Ash is the wood most often used for splints these days.

Reed, or fiber, splint is generally available in three widths: ½, ⅝, and ¾ inch. Since it is cut from the core of the rattan, each splint is quite long. The thin-width reed split totals about 130 feet long per coil. The widest reed splint runs about 60 feet to the coil. Some manufacturers make a reed splint with one side smoother than the other.

OTHER FIBERS USED FOR CANING

Sea grass

Sometimes called Hong Kong grass, sea grass is made by twisting grass into cord. The most popular size is #3, which is ³⁄₁₆ inch in diameter and is sold in coils about 300 feet long.

Fiber rush

Sometimes called genuine rush because it so closely resembles the real stuff originally made from marsh-grown flag (a kind of aquatic plant). Actually, it is genuine paper twisted to resemble rush.

Fiber rush comes in the following colors: golden brown, green, variegated, and yellow. The most popular size is #5, which is ⁵⁄₃₂ inch in diameter. It is sold in 2-pound coils.

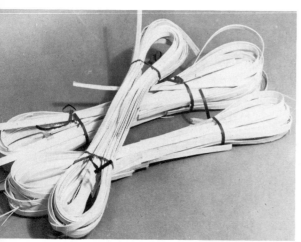

Coils of fiber splint. Each coil weighs one pound. Pictured splint is ½-inch wide. Each coil contains about 130 feet of splint.

A coil of sea grass. There is enough material here to cover an average chair bottom.

2
TOOLS AND EQUIPMENT

Very possibly you already have most or even all of the tools and equipment necessary for working with rattan, cane, reed, and other types of wicker. If you don't have any or all of the tools, don't rush out and buy them. You do not need all the tools listed for every job, and some craftsmen never use some of the tools for any work, for example, the long-nose and diagonal pliers.

Tools generally used with rattan are:

Large vise or equivalent	Old paintbrush
Workbench	Surform plane or coarse flat file
Large pan or bucket	Surform round file or coarse file
Hacksaw	Screwdriver
Propane torch	Long-nose pliers
Gas pliers	Diagonal cutting pliers
Electric or hand drill	C clamps
Drill bits, countersink	Spring clamps
6-foot rule	Try square/combination square
Hammer	Razor knife

Tool details

The vise must be large enough and strong enough to withstand a pull of a few hundred pounds. This is the torque (turning force) you will develop or exert when you tighten a length of rattan in the vise and push or pull the end of the rattan in your efforts to bend it. A clamp-on or a vacuum vise will not do. It must be bolted down with 1/4-inch or thicker lag bolts. Otherwise you will simply pull it free of the table when you work with 1-inch and thicker rattan poles.

You will need a strong vise mounted on a strong worktable in order to hold your rattan pole while you bend it. For cutting, almost any vise will do.

To prevent the jaws of the vise from marring the rattan, cover the jaws of the vise with several thicknesses of masking tape. Some craftsmen use strips of wood in place of the tape.

Since the vise can withstand no greater pull than the table to which it is fastened, you must have a strong workbench, and this should be bolted in place by one means or another. As an alternative to a strong workbench you can bolt your vise to any convenient timber in the basement or workroom, or you can bolt it to a Lally column in the basement. Just remember that all you need is something that will hold the rattan pole while you heat it and apply pressure.

As an alternative to purchasing a heavy-duty vise, you can use a pair of U bolts fastened to the top of your workbench. The bolts are positioned about 3 inches apart, parallel to each other and a few inches from the edge of the workbench. Use 3-inch bolts and position two strips of wood inside the bolts so that the rattan pole rests against the wood, not the metal.

To use the U-bolt vise simply slip the rattan inside the bolts and pull or push as necessary.

A low-cost alternative to a vise, useful mainly for bending purposes only, can be made by fastening two U bolts to a sturdy workbench. The pole to be bent is slid through the bolts. The strips of wood keep the bolts from marring the pole.

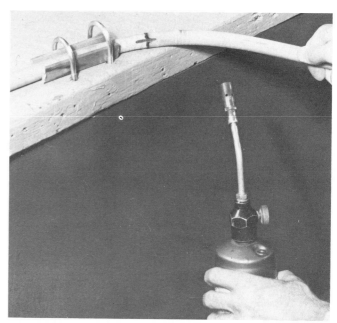

Use a propane torch for heating the rattan. Do not use a gasoline torch, even if you happen to have one on hand. The gasoline torches, though they supply more heat to a larger area, are dangerous and can explode. If you are purchasing a propane torch for this work, purchase a torch with a spreading nozzle, the nozzle that makes a wide flame. If you have a torch, the standard nozzle will do almost as well.

None of the other tools on the list deserves further mention; they are ordinary, everyday tools.

You will need a propane torch to bend the rattan. (Do not use an old gasoline blowtorch.) The standard nozzle shown is satisfactory, but if you are buying a nozzle, get the one that spreads the flame. It is better for rattan work.

Equipment for working with rattan

Unless you have an old wooden floor you don't mind marking up, or a large workbench, you will need an 8-foot plywood panel as a layout board. Any kind of plywood will do. Purchase the cheapest, $\frac{3}{8}$-inch-thick or thicker. The panel you will see in the photos further on in this book has been stained to make the photographs clearer. It is not a special panel.

In addition you will need some 6-penny common nails and scraps of wood, plus chalk and a length of rope.

Tools for working with cane, reed, etc.:
  Ruler
  Razor knife
  Hammer
  Spring clamp
  Screwdriver
  Caning awl (used for caning)
  Caning pegs
  Oiled hardwood wedges (use with cane webbing)
  Sea grass needle
  Rush shuttle (used with rush and fiber grass)

LEFT: You will find the Surform round file and the small plane more effective than either coarse files or rasps when working with rattan.

RIGHT: A spring clamp and a C clamp. You may or may not find them useful. Some craftsmen prefer to hold the parts together during assembly with wire, string, or masking tape. Some use all these plus the clamps.

Special tools   An electric drill (with bits) and an electric router are considered special simply because you will rarely need them when you are caning and working with reed.

You will need the drill when you clean out old caning holes that have become filled with varnish through the years. You will also need the drill to make holes in various pieces of furniture and basket bottoms and the likes when you want to use that portion of the furniture as a base for caning or the support of reed, as in the case of wicker furniture.

You will need the router and bit when you want to make a groove into which you can fasten cane webbing by means of a spline.

Though a ⅜-inch electric drill costs a little more, its slower, more powerful bit rotation is far more useful and effective than that of the ¼-inch drill.

While an electric drill is often useful around a home and workshop, and along with an assortment of bits can be purchased for under $25 today, routers cost several times more. And routers have little application outside of furniture making. It is therefore suggested that you not purchase a router and bit, but rent one when you need it.

Note that a router and bit have very little, if any, application in the making of rattan furniture. It is useful mainly for caning standard furniture and for repairing damaged cane seats and backs. Use of this tool is discussed in the last portion of this book, Part Three, Repairs.

3
CUTTING AND BENDING

CUTTING

Rattan is cut easily enough with almost any kind of saw. However, since rattan is covered with a hard, thin layer of silicon, ordinary wood saws do not hold their edge very long. It is therefore best to make your cuts with a hacksaw, using a fine-tooth blade. In most instances, when the rattan is up to 1 inch thick, you can make a reasonably square cut using your eye as a guide alone. When cutting thicker poles and a perfectly square cut is required, use a wood saw and a miter box.

Obviously, you will find it easiest to cut rattan while it is being held in a vise. But if you have instead a rattan holder made of U bolts, you can use that to hold the pole while you cut it.

PLANNING THE JOB FIRST

No particular planning is necessary before cutting a rattan pole that is going to be used as is, meaning that it is not going to be bent. But when the rattan is to be bent and curved, the picture changes. It is very difficult, even impossible to bend a piece of rattan or pipe, for that matter, to a predetermined shape without some sort of a guide. Just holding the bent and curved rattan up and looking at it won't work. No one's eye is accurate this way. On the other hand, it is comparatively easy to draw the shape you wish and then check its dimensions with a ruler, correcting as necessary.

Freehand

With a piece of chalk, sketch the curve you want on top of your workboard or workbench. Measure it to make certain it is the shape you wish and that it is as long as you want it to be.

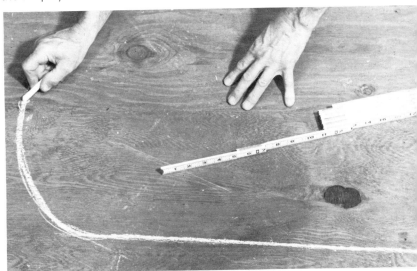

When you need a bent or curved section of rattan, plan, or lay out, the curve before you do any cutting or bending. Sketch the curve freehand, if you wish, using a ruler to check your dimensions.

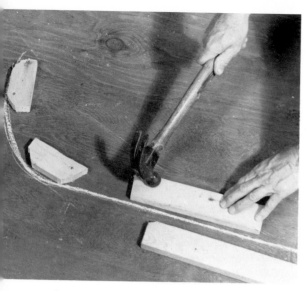

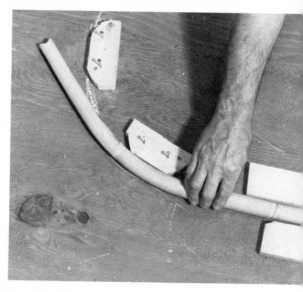

Outline the desired curve with pieces of scrap lumber nailed to your workboard. Bear in mind that the pole has thickness. Therefore you must allow for the thickness when you position the pieces of wood. The nailed-in-place pieces of wood now form a guide or gauge from which you can work.

As you bend the pole, keep trying it in your gauge. When it fits, you know you have the curve or shape you wish. Now, if there is no more bending to be done, you can cut it to length.

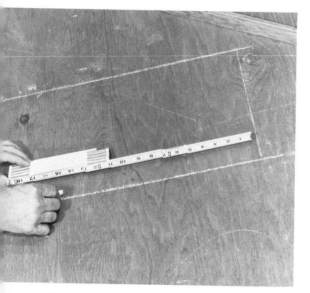

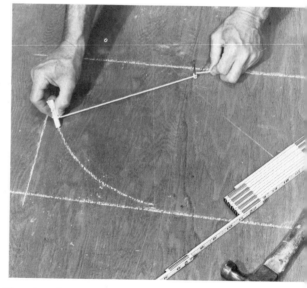

For more exact curves and shapes, lay out a square or rectangle.

Then draw the necessary arc within the outline with the aid of a compass made from a nail, a piece of string, and a piece of chalk. Then build your guide around the desired curved line.

Guides You can work to the chalk sketch alone if you wish, but you will find it easier if you fasten some guides to your workboard or workbench. Use scrap lumber, cut to a curve where necessary. Position the lumber to either side of your chalk line, leaving space for the width of the pole. Nail the guides in place. Now you have a go-no-go gauge. If your bent pole fits between the guides, its shape is correct. If not, you have to rebend the pole.

For more accurate shapes and arcs, lay out the job in a series of boxes or rectangles, drawn to exact size. Then freehand, or using a compass, fit the desired arcs into the boxes. You can make a compass from a piece of chalk, a piece of string, and a nail. Once drawn, you can position the guides as necessary.

Measuring the rattan When rattan or any material having thickness—as, for example, a pipe—is bent, its length is reduced. The exact amount its length diminishes can be computed by formula; but an easier way is to cut the rattan or pipe after you have bent it. If that is not practical, duplicate the path the bent rattan will follow with a piece of rope—in other words, lay the rope along the chalk line. Then mark the ends of the chalk line on the rope. Straighten out the rope. Measure it and you have the length of rattan necessary, but add a few inches to be on the safe side.

To find just how much pole length you need to go around a curve, stretch a piece of rope around the curve, then measure the rope.

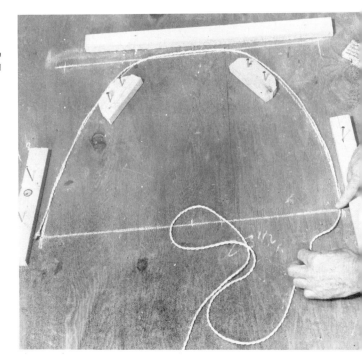

BENDING RATTAN

Rattan is very springy. It holds its shape much like steel and is probably as stiff as steel, pound for pound. As long as rattan is not forced beyond its natural resilience, it will return to its original shape. The engineering term for this is, of course, memory. Rattan has a strong or good memory. When it is forced beyond its natural resilience, the rattan assumes the new shape. In other words, the rattan is bent.

Rattan can be bent in any of three conditions: It can be bent as is, cold and dry. It can be bent after soaking. And it can be bent with the aid of heat and moisture.

Cold bending

Rattan is most difficult to bend when it is at room temperature and dry. In this condition a maximum amount of effort or pressure is required to change its shape. Also, in this condition, rattan is most easily damaged by bending. The thicker the pole, the more force necessary to bend it. But no matter what the pole thickness may be, force it too far and the fibers on the outside surface of the bend will tear loose and break. This happens readily with the thin poles but rarely with poles much more than ⅝ inch in diameter. With poles more than 1 inch in diameter it is almost impossible to do. So don't worry about damaging thick poles.

Cold bending is useful for straightening poles received from the supplier. Such poles are rarely perfectly straight, most of them retaining their original growth shapes.

Cold bending is also used to correct bends made by other methods. Cold bending is the method to use when all you want to do is alter a curve or bend just a little.

To cold-bend a pole, simply force it into the bend you wish. Since the rattan will not hold the bend but will straighten a little after you release it, it is necessary to overbend in order to secure the final results you want.

The degree of overbending necessary will vary with the diameter of the pole, the species, and the kind of bend you are introducing—gentle curve, sharp angle, or what have you. There is no formula for estimating the overbending necessary by any bending methods. You just have to try and see what happens.

If the pole is not too thick, you can change its shape a little by cold bending. Just force the pole to bend in the desired shape. The pole will tend to straighten after you let go, but some of the bend will permanently remain.

Thin poles can be bent by hand alone. Thicker poles need some sort of support to hold one end of the pole. If you have a strong vise attached to an equally strong workbench, use it. If not, find a hole in the foundation of your home into which you can poke the end of the pole while you pull on it. Or, possibly you can find two strong building timbers that will serve a like purpose.

If cold bending requires more force than you can muster, slip a section of galvanized iron pipe over the end of the pole. That will increase your leverage and the pressure you can put on the rattan pole.

Thin rattan is easily bent to a considerable degree without water or heat. Just be careful not to damage the pole when you overbend it.

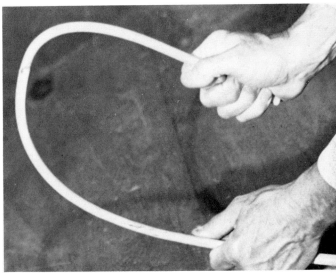

Cold, wet bending   Rattan ½ inch in diameter or so responds well to soaking, but it doesn't soak quickly. The rattan must be submerged for at least 24 hours for the soaking to be effective. More time is even better. Incidentally, if you place the merest pinch of detergent into the water, soaking will be more rapid or effective. (Detergent makes water more penetrating.) To fit a long pole into a small tub, roll the pole into a coil. Obviously this will not be possible with the thicker poles. With thin poles so coiled and soaked, you can readily shape them as desired while wet. If you allow the poles to dry while so coiled, you will, of course, find they hold the coiled shape.

Typically a ⅜-inch-thick rattan pole, which cannot be bent into a circle much under 7 inches in diameter when dry, can be bent into a 2¼-inch-diameter circle when thoroughly soaked. However, when you go past poles ½ inch in diameter or so, the beneficial effect of soaking upon bending falls off sharply. There is some easing of bend resistance when the rattan is waterlogged, but not much.

To keep a water-soaked pole from straightening out after it has dried, it must be held in the desired shape. Even so, upon drying the bent pole will to some degree return to its original shape. Therefore, you must overbend the wet rattan to compensate for the straightening. The degree of overbending necessary cannot be calculated. It has to be estimated.

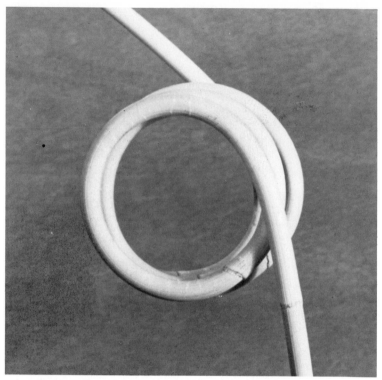

An example of what can be done by cold, wet bending alone. This piece of ⅜-inch rattan was soaked for a couple of days and then wrapped around a pipe. This is the shape the rattan held after drying and being removed from the pipe mandrel.

Pole diameter in inches	Diameter smallest circle in inches
⅜	2¼
½	3
⅝	4
¾	7
1	12
1¼	18
1½	26

Hot bending In order to bend rattan without damaging it, to an angle or arc with a smaller radius than possible when the rattan is dry or soaked, it is necessary to apply wet heat.

Rattan is a wood, and like most other woods it can be bent when hot and wet. Bent-wood chairs and planks fashioned for building the hulls of small boats are treated this way. But whereas commercial ship and furniture builders use steam boxes and hydraulic presses, individual rattan craftsmen use nothing more than a hand torch for heat and a brush to wet the rattan while it is being heated.

Setup for thick poles. Clamp one end of the pole in your vise or position it within the U bolts so that the start of the desired bend or curve is about 2 inches from the end of the vise or U bolts. Place a bowl of water and a paintbrush nearby. Check yourself to make certain you are wearing nothing that might swing or flap and get caught in the torch flame. Check the workbench and nearby area to make certain there is nothing flammable there or that, like paper, can be blown into the flame.

If you have stored your propane torch properly, you have stored the valve separately from the bottle. So now screw the valve portion onto the bottle. Open the valve and ignite the flame. Adjust the flame until it is of moderate size. You are now ready to begin hot bending.

Bending. Dip the brush into the water and wet the area of the rattan you plan to bend. Put the brush down and with one hand, pull or push the rattan as far as you can in the direction of the desired bend. With the other hand, play the torch flame over the area to be bent on the *inside* of the bend. Keep the torch flame moving slowly but constantly. When all the water has evaporated, continue applying the heat for a minute or so longer but not long enough to scorch the rattan. Put the torch down, apply some more water. Replace the brush and apply some more heat, all the time maintaining a steady pull or push on the rattan pole.

Continuing the pressure, repeat the wetting and heating. As you do so, you will feel the rattan soften somewhat and give a little. Keep the pressure on until you have overbent the pole a fair amount. The exact amount of overbending necessary will come with experience.

When you have bent the pole far enough to get behind it, you will be able to push it with your body. This will free both your hands so that you will be able to heat and wet without putting either tool down. Just be careful to keep the torch flame away from the brush. The flame can ignite the brush or melt it.

Controlling the bend. If you want a large radius, or gradual curve, swing your torch over a large section of the rattan. If you want a comparatively sharp bend or turn, confine the swing of the torch and the water to a small area. If a portion of the curve you are forming is still flat, concentrate a little more heat on that area. Just remember that the section of the pole that is hottest is going to bend the most.

Cooling. When you believe you have bent the pole sufficiently beyond the desired bend for the pole to assume the bend or curve you want, remove the torch flame and wet the rattan. Then, while still maintaining the pressure on the pole, wait a few minutes until the pole is cold enough to touch safely. Then release it. The pole will straighten a little, but the bend it retains when cold will be its new, permanent shape.

HOT BENDING A THICK POLE

The pole is clamped in the vise. That portion to be bent is made wet with the aid of a brush.

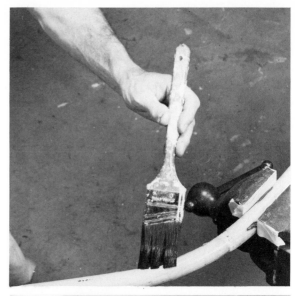

Heat is applied to the rattan with a torch. The tip of the torch is constantly moved from side to side to spread the heat and avoid burning the rattan. When the water on the rattan has evaporated, the heat is removed and more water is applied; then more heat is applied. Pressure is maintained on the pole all the time.

When the pole has been sufficiently bent for you to get behind it, do so, maintaining pressure on the pole by pushing your body against it. The advantage of using your body for pressure is that it leaves both hands free. You can apply water and heat alternately without allowing the pole to cool down.

Corrections. Remove the pole from the vise or U bolt and try it against your guides. If the bend is not correct, reheat it as before and apply pressure in the necessary direction and place to correct the bend. If all you need is a little correction, try correcting it cold first.

Burns and other damage. Whenever you bend rattan sharply, the layer of silicon on the inner side of the bend falls off. That makes this surface rough. This is normal and will be found on most commercial furniture.

When too much heat is concentrated on rattan, it naturally chars — it is, after all, a form of wood. Charring does not weaken the rattan, but it is unsightly. The simple solution, for both charring and a roughened inner surface where the silicon has fallen off is simply to sandpaper the area smooth and clean. Later the area should be varnished even if the rest of the piece is not.

Setup for thin poles. Stand your torch on your workbench. Ignite it. Hold the ends of the thin pole in your hand. Overbend the pole as required. In the case of a very small radius bend, you may have to bend the pole into a loop. Dip the section to be heated into a pan of water. Hold the bend over the flame until the water evaporates. Repeat the heating and wetting as long as necessary.

In order to bend short pieces of rattan without burning your hands, insert the ends of the rattan in pieces of pipe.

Everything mentioned previously in regard to hot-bending thick rattan poles applies to hot-bending thin poles.

This rattan can be bent without the help of a vise. Hold the rattan in the torch flame, as shown. Then dip the rattan into the bowl of water. To check quickly the progress of your bending, work over or close to a full-size drawing of the desired shape. This is the technique the natives of the Far East employ.

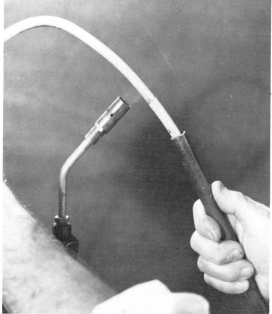

To secure more leverage or to hold the end of a piece of rattan near the flame, slip the end of the pole into a length of pipe. In this case a length of tubing was used. The pipe will not get hot if you keep it clear of the torch flame.

Native technique

The local craftsmen of Malaysia and similar areas squat on top of their layout boards when they bend small-diameter rattan. Then as they bend, they try the results against the sketch of the piece they are working on. This is not particularly important, but something that may be convenient for you.

WORKING WITH SKINNED RATTAN

Skinned, or shaved, rattan, as stated previously, is standard rattan from which the outer surface has been removed. Since this is removed with straight-edge knives, the surface of the skinned pole is not perfectly round but consists of a number of parallel flat surfaces.

So far as cutting and bending are concerned, skinned rattan can be treated exactly the same as standard, or unskinned, rattan. But since most of the hard surface is missing, skinned rattan is more responsive to water soaking, and it is more easily bent by any method. However, since some slivers of the hard surface are usually still present and since this does not bend as easily as the reed center of rattan, these slivers may be torn loose by bending. If this happens, just cut them free and sandpaper the surface smooth.

4
JOINTS

If you have never made more than a casual examination of rattan furniture, you may have accepted the obvious and believed that all rattan joints are held together by wrappings of cane. Perhaps the original rattan furniture was, the furniture made by the inhabitants of what is now Sri Lanka, Borneo, and Pago Pago, but the rattan furniture made for use in this country is not held together by cane wrapping alone. Furniture parts are joined by nails, screws, pegs, mortise-and-tenon joints, and glue. The wrappings are there mainly for decoration. The joint strength provided by the cane is usually unimportant.

TYPES OF JOINTS   There are approximately eight different basic types of joints. Whatever names are used to identify these joints in Sumatra, Micronesia, and Brooklyn are unimportant. What is important is that we understand one another, so I have given them names.

T joints. Two pieces of rattan meet to form the letter *T*. The horizontal portion of the T is called the crossbar. The vertical portion, the portion that terminates in the middle of the crossbar, is called the leg.

Angle joint. One piece of rattan is joined to the side of another at an angle.

Splice. Two pieces of rattan are joined to make a single length of rattan.

Folded joint. Two pieces of rattan are joined end to end to form an angle.

Corner joint. Two pole ends meet at another pole, as for example at a chair leg.

Parallel joint. A portion of two poles are joined to each other side by side.

Mortise-and-tenon joint. This is a standard carpentry joint. A hole is cut into the side of one piece of wood, and the end of the other is placed in the hole. Completed, it looks like a T joint.

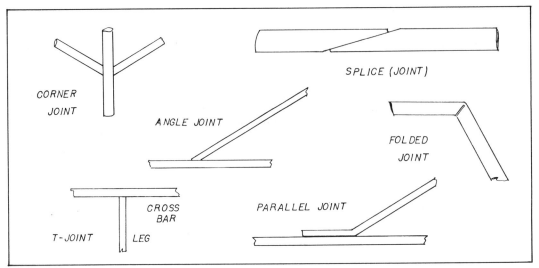

Basic types of joints most frequently used in the making of rattan furniture.

Pinned joint. A form of riveted joint.

T JOINTS

Shaping butted end

To form a T joint when working with rattan, the end of one pole is butted against the other. For a quick and easy-to-make joint, the butt end of the T leg is merely cut more or less square across.

For a much stronger and to some degree better looking joint, the butt end of the T leg is shaped into a concave arc that conforms to the roundness of the crossbar. This can be done by cutting a shallow V into the butt end with a hacksaw and then finishing up with a coarse rat-tail file or a Surform round file.

Two things must be kept in mind when you curve the butt end of the T leg: One, the concave curve shortens the rattan pole by a distance equal to the depth of the curve. (Twice this distance if you curve both ends of the same pole.) Two, you must align the concave curves with the length of the poles they will join.

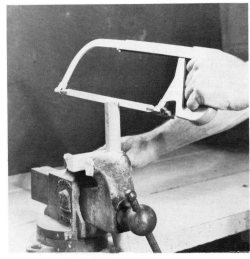

Neater, closer-fitting T joints are made by chamfering (grooving) the end of the leg to fit the crossbar. To save time, the first step consists of hacksawing a V in the end of the leg.

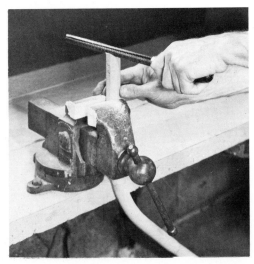

The V cut is shaped to match the side of the crossbar with the aid of a Surform round file, or a standard round file.

Nails or screws? To nail, simply drive a 6-penny or larger common nail through the side of one pole and into the center of the butt end of the T-leg pole.

A nail joint has moderate strength, but it must be wrapped, as shall be described shortly. Otherwise, it is possible for the nail to work its way out of the joint.

For a fast T joint, a nail is simply driven through the crossbar and into the end of the leg. This leg end has not been chamfered.

A screw joint is far stronger and doesn't need to be wrapped. On some commercial furniture no joints are wrapped. Flathead brass screws are used and left exposed. To use a screw for the joint, drill and countersink a hole through the crossbar portion of the joint and partway into the butt end of the T leg. (Countersinking means cutting a circular depression at the top of the hole, which allows the head of the screw to be lower than the surface of the wood.)

To save time use a wood screw pilot drill. This drill both cuts the pilot hole for the screw and countersinks the top of the wood at the same time. But you must use a pilot drill that matches the screw's size.

Use #8 or #10 flathead wood screws sufficiently long to penetrate the butt end of the pole at least ¾ inch on poles up to ¾ inch thick; more on thicker poles. Note that the #10 screws are thicker than the #8's.

Brass screws are nice if you want to go to the expense, but they are unnecessary if you plan to wrap the joints. If you are concerned that iron screw heads may rust, and the rust create a stain with time, place a dollop of Duco cement on top of each screw head. The cement will seal the moisture out.

32

For a strong joint, the leg end is chamfered and a hole is drilled through the crossbar.

Then a screw is driven through the hole and into the end of the leg. The screw should be long enough to go into the leg for at least ¾ inch.

ANGLE JOINTS   To make an angle joint, cut the end of one pole at an angle that will permit the pole to form the desired angle with the other pole. The length of the cut should be at least 1½ inches long. If the angle or pole's lack of thickness is such that this cannot be done, think about using a T joint in its place or possibly using a parallel joint and bending the thinner pole after the joint.

For maximum angle-joint strength, file a flat area on the uncut pole where the two poles join. If the joint is merely ornamental, you can use some thin nails to hold the pieces of rattan together. If there is going to be any load (pressure), it is best to use wood screws.

Making an angle joint.

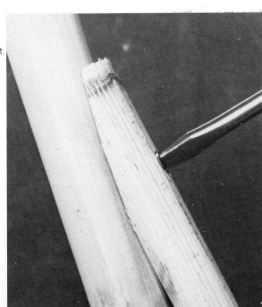

SPLICES   Cut the ends of the two poles to be joined at matching angles. Make the angles long enough to permit one pole to overlap the other by 2 inches or more.

When joining ornamental poles less than ½ inch in diameter or so, place glue on the mating surfaces and drive 1-inch nails through both poles. Bend the nail ends back on themselves if necessary. Two nails should be plenty.

When joining thicker poles that are to be part of an assembly structure and will be subjected to a load, use wood glue plus wood screws at the joint. For maximum strength use bolts, but countersink both ends of the bolt holes so that both the bolt heads and bolt nuts are below the surface of the rattan poles.

Although screwed or bolted splices are very strong, the joint area is not flexible. You can bend a splice a little, but you cannot curve it or bend it as you can the rest of the rattan poles. If you have to join short poles to make a long one and must put a deep bend in the long pole, plan your work so that the bend occurs away from the splice.

 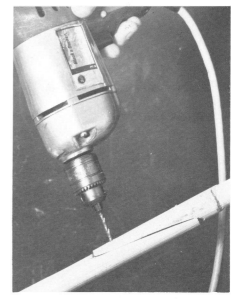

MAKING A SPLICE

ABOVE LEFT: A long angle is cut on the two ends of the poles to be spliced.

ABOVE RIGHT: The two angled ends of the two poles are positioned one above the other. Holes for screws are drilled through the upper pole. Glue is placed on the facing surfaces.

RIGHT: Screws are driven through the holes. The screws and glue hold the pole ends permanently together.

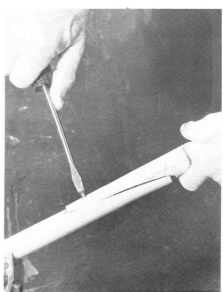

FOLDED, OR BENT, JOINTS   A folded joint can be made two ways. You can cut the ends of two poles at an angle. Put the pole ends together and fasten them with nails and glue or screws and glue.

The better way utilizes a single pole. With a hacksaw a triangular section of rattan is removed from the side of the pole at the point it is to be folded. The two cuts necessary to free the piece of wood are angled exactly as you wish the resultant joint to be. The cuts almost sever the pole. The piece of rattan remaining serves as a hinge.

MAKING A FOLDED JOINT

A wedge is cut out of the pole at the exact point the angle is desired. The sides of the wedge or the sides of the cut must equal the desired angle of the completed joint.

Next the hinge is wetted down, heated, and bent. If the resultant angle is not what you need, file away some of the rattan inside the joint or add a thick layer of plastic wood.

The rattan pole is then bent at the thin portion of the cut. To make certain the rattan does not rip or break as this bend is made, it is best to use wet heat while bending.

When you have the folded angle you wish, drill through one portion of the joint into the other and drive a long wood screw home. Cover the screw head with a little pale brown plastic wood or putty. You can also use a finishing nail here, but it is not as strong. However, you can hide its head easily enough by merely driving it below the surface of the rattan.

Folded joints are not wrapped. There appears to be no practical way of doing this.

A hole is drilled through one portion of the joint directly into the end of the other portion of the joint. Then a long wood screw is used to hold the joint closed.

CORNER JOINTS   A corner joint can be considered as two T joints having a single, common crossbar. The only problem that arises is that of using wood screws to fasten the T legs to the crossbar.

If you use nails to fasten the T legs, it is easy enough to position one nail higher than the other so that they can pass each other going through the crossbar without problem. If you use wood screws, the same technique is used — one screw above the other, but since they are thicker, you will find it easier if you angle the screws away from each other as well as trying to space them apart. Still, when working with thin poles, it is not easy.

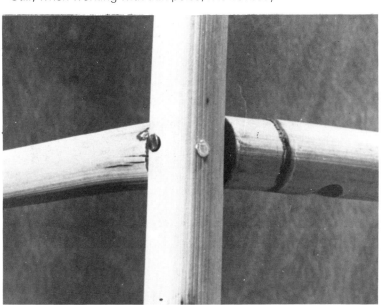

Typical corner joint.

PARALLEL JOINTS   Parallel joints are used to fasten the side of one pole to the side of another. These joints usually find application when a thin pole must be fastened to a thick pole. Generally, the thin pole is bent sharply away from the thick pole at a right angle shortly after the joint. For example, if you are going to make the back of a chaise out of a 1-inch-thick frame and want to have a lot of parallel ½-inch poles crossing the frame, the ½-inch stuff would be joined to the 1-inch frame by means of parallel joints. Each joint might be 2 inches long, after which the thin pole would angle sharply away from the thick pole.

Parallel joints are usually made with a little glue and some nails because they usually carry no or little load. And they are usually wrapped, and in this case the wrapping can and does provide much of the required strength.

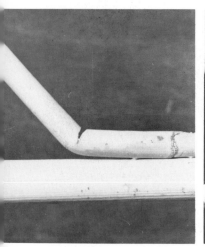 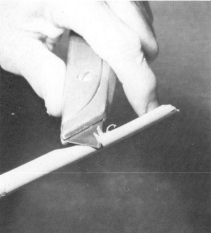 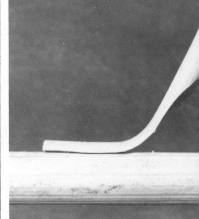

TWO TYPES OF PARALLEL JOINTS

LEFT: A notch is cut into the side of the rattan. The short end of the rattan is nailed or screwed down. Then the other end of the rattan is angled off as necessary.

CENTER: A section is cut off the side of a piece of rattan.

RIGHT: The thin portion of the rattan is nailed down. The rest of the rattan can be bent away as required.

MORTISE-AND-TENON JOINTS   Because of the obvious parallel to sexual anatomy, you can call the tenon portion of the joint male and the mortise female. These joints offer maximum strength and should be used where you expect great pressure against the side of the T-leg portion of the joint. For example, mortise-and-tenon joints would keep a chair's rung from pulling free when some boor put his or her full weight on it.

Start by tapering the end of the pole that is to be used for the T leg of the joint. Select a wood drill or twist drill bit to match the diameter of the tapered pole end. Drill into the other pole (the crossbar) no more than one-half its diameter. Try the pole end in the hole for size. If it's too loose, file the pole a bit shorter. If too tight, taper some more. When the fit is snug, drill a pilot hole through the crossbar pole from the other side, then, after you have put a little glue in the large hole and inserted the tapered pole end, drive a screw through the pilot hole and into the pole end.

Mortise-and-tenon joints do not have to be wrapped. They are strong and attractive. But although these joints are easy to make, they require more care when the T leg is to be fitted between two crossbar poles, as, for example, when you are making a rung for a chair.

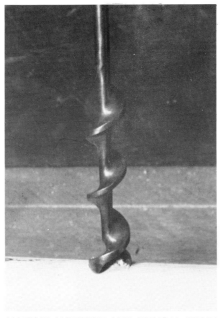

MAKING MORTISE-AND-TENON JOINT

A hole is drilled into the crossbar

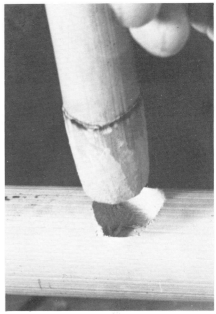

The end of the T leg is tapered. Glue is placed in the hole. The tenon (leg) is forced into the hole. A screw driven into the leg from the other side of the crossbar holds the leg in place. This is the strongest kind of joint that is normally used with rattan furniture

PINNED JOINTS   A pinned rattan joint is a form of riveted joint. Real rivets, however, cannot be used with rattan, since the process of heading the rivet would mash the wood. Thus a pinned rattan joint utilizes a rivet without a head. This can be a nail that is cut short before or after insertion or even a short piece of reed.

A hole is drilled through both pieces of rattan. The cut-short nail or piece of reed is slipped through the holes along with a little cement. In the case of a reed or even wood rivet, the cement will hold it in place. Nothing more need be done except to make the ends of the rivet flush with the surfaces of the rattan. In the case of the nail it is necessary to wrap the joint, taking care to make certain the cane not only hides the nail but also holds it in place.

Pinned joints can be comparatively easily pulled apart. But they have tremendous cross-pull resistance. In the case of the nail, the rattan will give way before the nail will shear in half.

If the design calls for great strength in all directions, use a nut and bolt in place of the rivet. Countersink both ends of the hole so that the bolt head and nut are below the surface of the rattan. Then hide the bolt with a little putty.

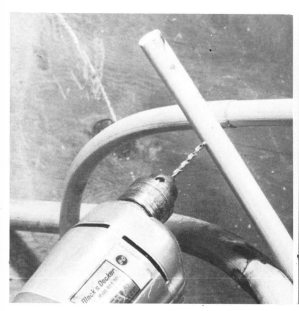

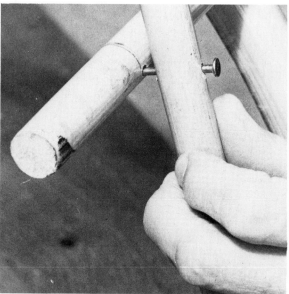

MAKING A PINNED JOINT

A hole is drilled through both pieces of rattan that are to be pinned (joined).

A pin of some kind is then slipped through the holes in the two pieces of rattan. If a nail, as illustrated, is used, it has to be cut short and held in place by cane wrapping. If a piece of reed or dowel is used, glue alone will usually do.

WRAPPING
Many rattan joints are wrapped. It is tradition, and it is expected. But not all rattan joints are wrapped. Many modern furniture designers omit all wrapping. And some rattan joints cannot be neatly wrapped. One example, previously mentioned, is the bent, or folded, joint. No one has yet found a way to wrap this joint and make it look right. So it is not wrapped.

In any event, wrapping is usually done with wide cane called wrapping cane, which is 6 to 6½ mm wide. Any of a number of methods or techniques are used. Some are faster than others; some produce neater joints, and some resist the efforts of children and little dogs better than others.

Cane length
Since it is an awful nuisance to thread a long length of cane around and around a pole, it is nice to know in advance just

how long a piece of cane is needed for a particular wrap. The formula below will help you find this valuable figure.

Required cane length = number of turns × 4 × pole diameter in inches (or fraction of an inch) + 8 inches.

To find number of needed turns, multiply the desired length of the wrap, in inches, by 4.

The 8 inches is a fudge figure. It is added to make certain you have enough, and also to provide a grip on the cane.

Preparing the cane   Soak the cane in warm or lukewarm water for at least 20 minutes prior to using. Dampen every now and again, since the cane dries very quickly. Wet cane bends and binds well. Dry cane cracks and tends to split. When gluing, you can use white glue on wet or dry cane. Use Duco cement on dry cane only.

To determine approximately how much cane you require to wrap a particular joint, find the number of turns needed by multiplying the length of the desired wrap in inches by 4. Multiply this number by a second 4 and then again by the pole diameter in inches. To this, add 8 inches.

For example, you want 2 inches of wrap on a 1-inch diameter pole.

```
2 inches of wrap X 4  =   8
            8 X 4  =  32
  32 X 1 (diam.)   =  32
         32 + 8    =  40 inches
```

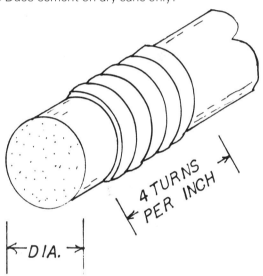

A tip on nailing cane   Some craftsmen find that it saves time to start a nail through the cane before they attempt to nail the cane to a pole. Very simply, the cane is positioned atop the workbench and the nail is driven through the cane end—at least ½ inch away from the end to prevent it from splitting. Then the cane—with the nail near its end—is positioned and the nail driven home.

When fastening the other end of the cane in place, some craftsmen use a pair of long-nose pliers to hold the nail while they hammer it.

Keeping it wet   Note that while you can work with cane that is dry, you will secure tighter turns and tighter knots and there will be less splitting from nailing when you soak the cane prior to using it and keep it wet while you work. But let it dry before you apply cement.

Nails-only method   Nail one end of the cane to the pole with a ½-inch #20 wire nail. (Nails are thinner than brads.)

Complete the wrap by wrapping the cane tightly around the rattan pole for as many turns as you wish or need. Then, hold the cane tightly in place, nail its end down, and cut off the excess, again leaving at least ½ inch of cane beyond the nail. The nailed wrapping looks good if the nails are positioned out of sight.

Unfortunately, the wrapping is easily knocked loose and this method of holding the cane in place is not advisable where it may be struck while the furniture is in use. It is perfectly satisfactory in positions where it will not normally be struck.

The easy way to nail the end of a piece of cane to the pole is to place the cane on a soft board, drive the nail through the cane, then lift the cane and nail, as shown. Now you can position the cane end and nail where you wish on the pole.

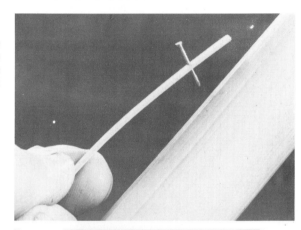

This is what a nailed-in-place cane wrapping looks like. The second nail has been started. It will now be made snug. Do not drive the nail home or you will split the cane.

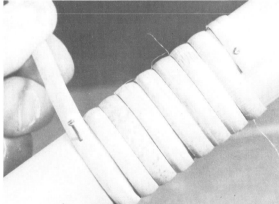

The extra cane can now be cut off with a razor knife, as shown, or with a pair of diagonal pliers.

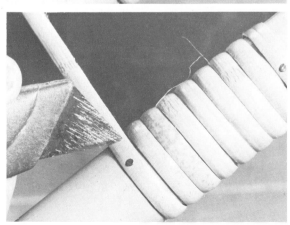

Knotted wrapping
Start either by making a knot in the cane or by merely slipping the end of the cane under the first two or three turns. Finish by holding the last two turns a distance away from the balance of the turns. Then slip the end of the cane under the last two turns and pull up tight. Then push the turns against one another to make a close wrap.

This method is fast and easy and, like the nails-only method, good where little or no traffic contact is expected. However, its surface is a bit lumpy—due to the knots—in comparison with the nailed method.

USING KNOTS AND GLUE TO HOLD CANE WRAPPING IN PLACE

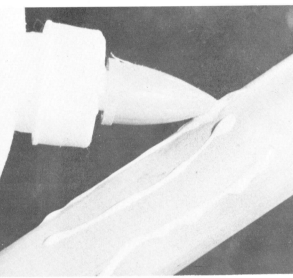

Glue is applied to the rattan pole.

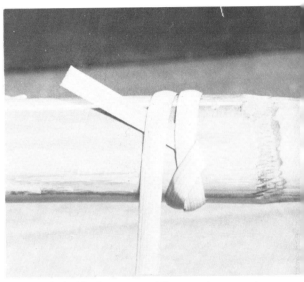

A knot is tied in the cane and the cane is wrapped around the rattan.

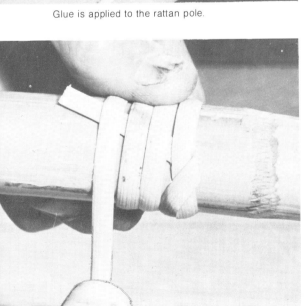

Wrapping is continued.

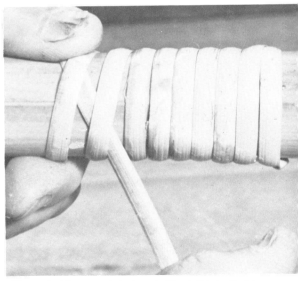

The end of the cane is fastened with another knot and pulled tight.

Knots and glue   Start by covering the area to be wrapped with a good glue. Elmer's will do fine. Then knot the wrap as before. When done, wipe the excess glue off with a damp cloth.

Or, omit the glue at the start. Knot and wrap as before. When completed, let the wrapping dry overnight. Then, when the cane is perfectly dry, force Duco or similar cement beneath the wrapping.

Both methods result in very tight and fairly permanently positioned wrappings. However, the glue-first method is mucky and the cement-later method leaves visible lumps of cement.

USING KNOTS AND CEMENT TO HOLD CANE WRAPPING IN PLACE

 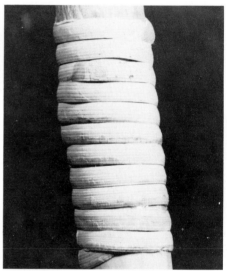

The wrapping is applied and fastened using knots alone. The cane is given a day to dry completely. Then cement is forced between the cane and the pole.

Close-up of a wrapping held in place by knots and glue or cement. The surface of the wrap is uneven, and you can more or less see where the knots are.

Knots and nails   This method requires a little more effort but results in a wrap that cannot be accidentally removed. If you want to remove this wrapping, you have to cut it off.

Start by nailing the end of the cane more or less lengthwise to the rattan. Then wrap over the nail and the end of the cane. Finish up as if you were merely going to knot the end, but before you push the last turns in place, nail the end of the cane down. Trim it with a razor knife and then push the last turns over the second nail.

USING KNOTS AND NAILS TO HOLD
THE WRAPPING IN PLACE

The starting end of the cane is nailed to the pole. Wrapping is now done in the direction of the thumb so as to wrap the cane over the nail.

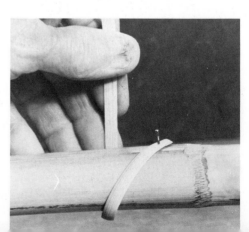

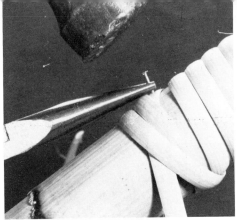
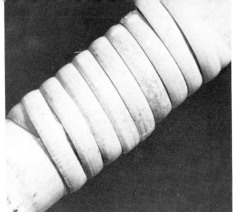

A knot is made at the end of the wrap. Note how the end of the cane has been slipped beneath the last two turns. A nail is now driven through the cane, as shown. The use of long-nose pliers here eases the task considerably.

The extra cane is cut off and the cane turns are pushed together and up and over the nail.

Pegs
Except for the nails-only method, the other methods described leave a somewhat lumpy surface. The pegged method, however, leaves a very smooth finished surface that will never come loose, do what you may.

Start by drilling a ⅛-inch-diameter hole about ½ inch deep into the pole. Fold the end of the cane lengthwise—you may have to split it to do this—and poke the folded cane end into the hole. Now wrap the cane around the pole. When you reach the desired end of the wrapping, drill another hole ⅛-inch through the pole all the way through. With the razor knife shave off the sides of the cane so that you can force it through the hole. Then, using a pair of pliers, pull the protruding cane end as tight as you can. Cut off the excess cane flush with the side of the pole.

Another method consists of drilling the two holes first and adjusting the wrapping as may be necessary to accommodate the hole spacing.

If you wish, you can simply let the wrapping be. It won't come loose. Or, you can put a drop of cement in the holes. Or you can actually peg them with dowel. Or you can fill the holes with putty. For perfection, color the putty with a little ocher oil paint to match the color of the rattan.

PEGGED WRAPPINGS

Drill a ⅛-inch-diameter hole ½ inch deep into the pole.

Force the end of the cane into the hole.

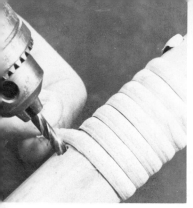 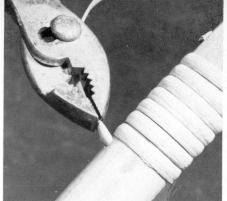 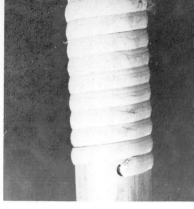

LEFT: Wrap the cane around the pole. Then drill a ⅛-inch hole alongside the cane and completely through the rattan pole.

CENTER: Force the end of the cane through the hole and pull it tight with the help of pliers. Cut the end of the protruding cane flush with the surface of the pole.

RIGHT: This is what the finished wrapping looks like. This method takes the most time but it produces the best results in strength and appearance.

Wrapping T joints

Start by cutting a number of pieces of cane about 7 inches long. Use sufficient cane strips to cover the thickness of the T leg. Since four pieces of wrapping cane side by side amounts to 1 inch, figure one cane for every ¼ inch of pole diameter. More will do no harm. Nail the canes side by side to the T leg, positioned so that about half the length of the cane pieces projects beyond the joint's crossbar. Use the ½-inch #20 nails mentioned previously. Fold the cane over the crossbar. Nail the free cane ends to the side of the T leg.

Next you have to wrap the T leg. Start ½ inch or so clear of the cut ends of the cane. Continue wrapping right over the canes until you are close to the crossbar. Then tie off the wrapping cane by any of the methods already discussed.

As you can see, the parallel canes hide the nail or screw head used to make the T joint, hide the joint between the butt end of the T leg and the crossbar, and give the joint a finished "rattan" appearance.

WRAPPING A T JOINT

LEFT: Cut a number of pieces of cane. Nail them to the leg of the joint side by side, as shown.

CENTER: Fold the cane up and over the crossbar of the joint. Nail the cane to the other side of the joint leg, as shown.

RIGHT: Now cover the ends of the cut-and-nailed cane with a simple wrap. Finish the wrapping off with a knot, as shown, or use any other of the suggested methods.

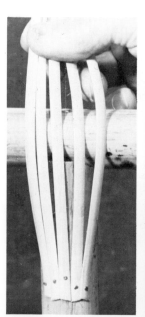  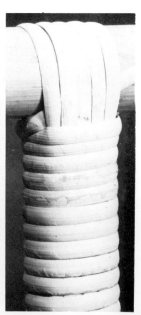

Angle joints   Begin your wrapping on the thicker or main pole about ½ inch or so beyond the end of the second pole. Or, begin your wrapping flush with the end of the second pole. In either case, continue wrapping both poles until the space between the poles (where one bends away from the other) is more than ½ inch or so. Then tie off the cane. The reason for not wrapping any further is merely appearance.

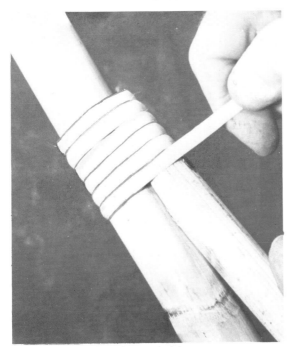
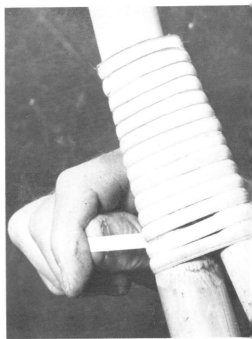

Starting the wrapping of an angle joint.   Completing the wrapping of an angle joint.

Splices   Use the same technique suggested for wrapping angle joints.

Folded joints   If you can figure out how to wrap these joints without the cane slipping off, go to it. You will be making rattan history. So far, no one has come up with a neat, attractive technique for wrapping folded joints. So they aren't wrapped.

Corner joints   Cut as many pieces of cane as you would cut for an ordinary T joint, with each piece about 7 inches long. Forget the second T leg for the moment and nail the pieces of cane onto the outside of the first T leg, as suggested for wrapping a T joint previously. Bend the pieces of cane around the crossbar and nail the ends onto the second T leg. Now cut an equal number of additional pieces of cane about 6 inches long. Go to the inside of the first T leg. Nail the cane in position. Use masking tape or some string to force the canes against the crossbar. Nail the ends of the second canes to the second T leg.

Start your wrapping on either T leg and continue on over the crossbar and down the other leg. With a little care you can position the cane out of sight where it goes over the crossbar. Tie off the end of the cane when you have completed wrapping all the parallel canes on the T leg. If you wish, you can wrap each T leg separately, tying off the cane as it reaches the crossbar.

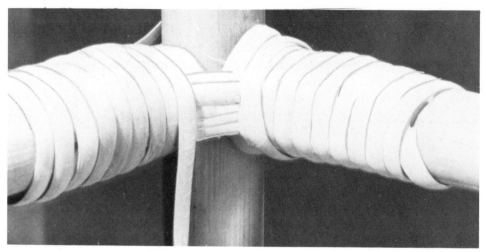

Wrapping a corner joint.

5
ORNAMENTATION

For the purpose of discussion, we shall call any and all materials added permanently to an otherwise complete piece of furniture an ornamentation. Thus a curl of reed fastened to a chaise is an ornamentation. A beautiful woman draped over, or handsome man lounging on, the same piece of furniture is not an ornament, but a pleasure.

Cane, reed, split and small-diameter rattan are the materials most used. Not only are they comparatively easy to shape and fashion, they naturally blend well with rattan furniture. Other materials do not suit rattan furniture and are therefore seldom if ever used.

CANE   In the previous chapter the use of cane as a wrapping and binding material was discussed. The same cane and the same methods and techniques are also used for ornamentation.

Treating pole ends   You can let a pole end remain in the condition you find it — slashed by a jungle rattan farmer's bolo or whatever — or you can saw it neatly across. Or you can round it off a bit with a file or Surform plane. You will find that many furniture designers and makers do nothing more. But some bind the pole ends. The choice is yours.

To bind a pole end — this is difficult to do with poles much under an inch in diameter — nail pieces of cane over the end of the pole and then wrap the ends of the pieces and the nails with more cane.

Nail the first piece of cane to the pole about 4 or so inches from the pole end. Bend the cane over the pole end and nail it to the other side of the pole. Nail the second piece of cane alongside the first. Do the same with the third. Now you are going to have trouble nailing the fourth and following pieces of cane parallel to the first. There won't be room for them all at the end of the pole. So, the fourth piece of cane and the following piece are positioned alongside each other at the sides of the pole, they cross over the first three canes at the end of the pole.

Now, depending on the width of the cane used and the diameter of the pole, you may have bare pole showing between canes. Cover any bare area by inserting pieces of cane between the nailed canes.

To finish, start a cane wrap about 1 inch below the nails, or below the ends of the canes. Wrap over the nail ends and about 1 inch beyond; then tie off the cane by one method or another. To keep the cane at the end of the pole from moving, force some cement between the canes and the pole end.

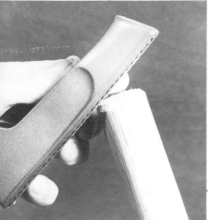

WRAPPING A POLE END

LEFT: Round the pole end with a file or Surform plane.

CENTER: Cover the end with pieces of cane nailed side by side. Fill the open spaces with short pieces forced into place. They do not have to be nailed.

RIGHT: Wrap the pole as shown, leaving some of the cane that is folded over the pole end visible. Let the cane dry. Force cement between the canes to hold everything in place.

Spaced wrappings

When the furniture includes several long straight rattan poles and they appear bare and unappealing, spaced wrappings are often used to make them visually more interesting. Each wrap is made several inches long and applied by the same methods and techniques previously described. The wrappings are spaced equidistant from one another and the ends or terminations of the poles.

MAKING AN ORNAMENTAL DIAMOND PATTERN ON A POLE

Wrap the cane in a wide spiral, as shown. Nail the start of the cane and where you wish to start the return wrap.

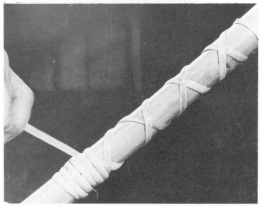

Bring the cane back to its starting point, as shown. Then wrap the starting point, as shown. Next the other end of the diamond pattern is wrapped.

Wrappings that hide Sometimes it is necessary to use sections of common wood and skinned rattan when making wicker and rattan furniture. Neither of these two materials blends well with wicker or rattan furniture. A commonly used technique to hide these materials is to wrap them completely in cane.

The procedure is the same as that already described. You simply start at one end of the piece of wood or skinned rattan and wrap until it is completely covered, whereupon you fasten the end of the cane. In many cases you will find yourself struggling to control yards of cane as you circle it around the wood or skinned rattan you are wrapping. To avoid this, you can cut the cane into reasonable lengths and start the second and following piece of cane by nailing and gluing it atop the end of the previously positioned cane. Just take care to make these splices out of sight.

Using cane to hide. In this case the raw edge of a strip of plywood is hidden with a wrapping of cane. Cane is often used to hide skinned rattan.

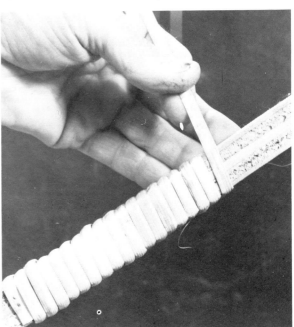

Spiral wrappings Start by nailing the cane to the pole. Continue by wrapping the cane around the pole. But, instead of keeping the turns close to one another, space them out so that the cane spirals around the pole. Terminate by nailing the cane end to the pole.

Next, return to the start of the cane. Give the pole a half turn. Start a second cane directly opposite the start of the first cane. In other words, if you were to drill a hole straight through the pole, the hole would be beneath both starting ends of the two canes. Now spiral the second cane around the pole taking care to keep the spacing between the turns of the second cane equal to the spacing between turns of the first cane. You will know they are correct when the crossed spirals look good. Nail the end of the second cane in place.

Return to the start of the two canes. Wrap this area with four or five turns of closely spaced cane. This hides the nailed ends and gives the spiral wrappings a finished appearance. Do the same at the other end, using the same number of turns.

There are any number of variations to the basic spiral wrap. One is to work both canes at the same time and overlap them alternately, much like weaving. Another is to use two parallel canes in place of each single cane, thus doubling the width of the spiraling canes. Still another is to use four individual canes, spaced at quarter turns around the circumference of the pole.

REED

As stated previously, reed is the central core of the rattan palm. Like rattan, reed can be bent to some degree when dry, but not much. You have to overbend to make it hold the bend, but if you overbend too much, like rattan it will splinter.

However, when reed is soaked in lukewarm water for 20 minutes or so (depending on its thickness), it becomes very pliant—so pliant that it can almost be bent back upon itself without damage. If the reed is held in its bent shape until it is bone dry, it will hold its shape with just a little self-straightening.

Reed may be fastened to portions of the furniture by glue, cement, nails, cane wrappings, and by slipping the reed through holes in the furniture. This latter technique is often used in making wicker furniture. The reed is supported by a number of holes drilled through the frame.

Independent circles

Start by soaking the reed and then wrapping it around a section of pipe or even a tin can having a diameter approximately one-third less than the desired internal diameter of the completed circle you wish to construct. Use rubber bands or string to hold the reed tightly and evenly in place around the pipe that serves as a mandrel. Next, place the pipe and reed in water. Let it soak awhile—generally, twenty minutes suffices. Remove the pipe and reed and work the reed with your fingers to make certain it is not more tightly wound at one point on the mandrel than at another. Return the reed and mandrel to the water and let it soak for an hour or more.

Remove the mandrel and reed from the water and let the reed dry on the mandrel. Give it plenty of time—you want the reed bone dry.

Remove the dry reed from the mandrel. You now have a coil of reed with an internal diameter close to what you need. With a razor knife cut the reed into circles, taking care to make each cut square across the reed.

Place a circle of reed in a vise. Drive half the length of a nail into one end of the reed. Cut the nail head off. (A pair of diagonal pliers is just the tool to use.) Place a drop of Duco cement on the nail and reed end. Force the other end of the reed down on the nail until the two ends meet. Let the cement harden and you have a ring of reed.

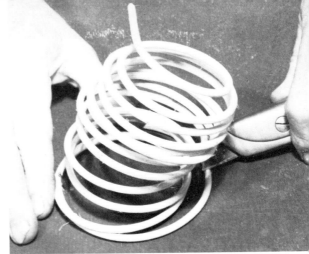
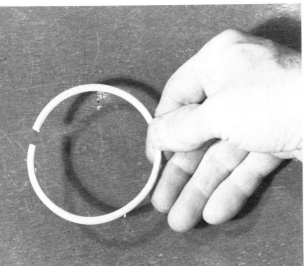

MAKING INDEPENDENT CIRCLES OF REED

TOP LEFT: The reed is soaked, wrapped tightly around a form or mandrel, smaller in diameter than the desired final circle diameter. Then the reed on its mandrel is soaked for a half hour or so. They are removed and the reed is permitted to dry thoroughly.

TOP RIGHT: When the reed is bone dry, it is removed from the mandrel and a razor knife is used to cut a circle of reed from the coil.

BOTTOM LEFT: This is what the cut circle of reed looks like. Now it is necessary to join its two ends permanently.

BOTTOM RIGHT: A small nail is forced into one end of the reed. The head of the nail is cut off. The cut end of the nail is forced into the other end of the reed. Before the two reed ends are forced completely together, a drop of cement is placed between them. This locks the ends together.

Adjoining circles   Make a number of independent circles, as just suggested. Temporarily fasten the circles side to side with masking tape. Position the circles on the rattan pole or whatever you wish to ornament. Next, fasten the circles to the pole. Do this with nails and cement or nails, cement, and cane wrappings. Remove the masking tape. If desired or necessary, cement the edges of the circles to each other. To keep them in line, clamp them between two pieces of wood until the cement hardens. (To keep the circles from adhering to the clamps, cover the strips of wood with wax paper.)

Continuous circles

(If you remember your penmanship classes, this was one of the exercises—you drew a series of circles without lifting your pen.) Shape the reed on a mandrel, as suggested. Pull the dry coil of reed sideways so as to produce a string of circles.

Fasten two strips of wood to your workboard, parallel to each other and just as far apart as the overall height of your circles. Position the pulled-out coil of reed between the guides. Fasten one end of the coil to the board. Stretch the coil; adjust each turn; fasten the end of the coil to the board. Place some cement at the points where the reed touches itself. Place a flat board atop the circles. When the cement dries, you can remove the reed. You will have a series of continuous, overlapping circles, which you can fasten in place by any of the methods suggested.

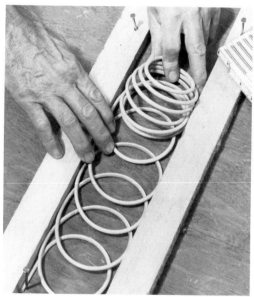 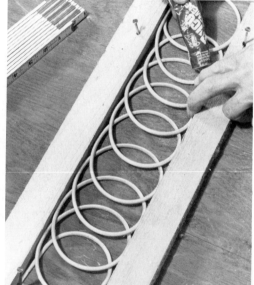

MAKING CONTINUOUS CIRCLES OF REED

ABOVE LEFT: Shape the reed on a mandrel. Pull the dry coil of reed sideways so as to produce a string of circles. Place the string of circles between two guides.

ABOVE RIGHT: Fasten one circle to another with drops of cement. Place a board atop the string of circles.

RIGHT: This is what you have when the cement dries.

Diminishing-diameter circles
The previous techniques produce a series of circles of the same diameter. But you can also produce a row of circles that become increasingly smaller in diameter.

Start by placing two strips of wood on the top of your workboard or bench. Nail one board lightly in place. (Don't drive the nails home.) Position the second so that one end is as close to the first board as you wish the diameter of the smallest circle in the series to be. Position the other end of the second board so that it is just as far away from the first as you wish the diameter of the largest circle to be. Nail the second board lightly in place.

Next, fasten one end of a well-soaked coil of reed to one strip of wood. Form the reed into a series of adjoining curls or circles. Space the circles evenly apart and make them just fit between the two guides. Fasten the other end of the reed to the other guide. Place a third board on top of the reed curls to hold them down. Let the reed dry thoroughly. Apply a few drops of cement between adjoining sections of the reed. Let the cement dry. Now you can lift the ornament out of its guides and fasten it in place where you wish.

MAKING DIMINISHING-DIAMETER
CIRCLES OF REED

Fashion a guide as shown.

Position well-soaked reed between the guides, as shown, to make the desired adjoining circles.

Let the reed dry thoroughly. Then apply cement between adjoining reed circles.

Place a board atop the reed so that it will hold its position until the cement dries.

This is what the dry reed and cement look like when removed from the guide.

This is how the circles look when fastened to a pole. The masking tape will be covered by the cane wrapping.

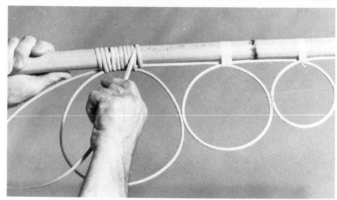

Semicircles

Semicircle ornamentation is made by forming the reed into a coil of the desired diameter by soaking it and permitting it to dry on a form. Then the reed is cut into semicircles and nailed to the side of the supporting member.

Waves

Circle ornamentation starts with a coil of reed that can then be pulled apart and stretched out. The reed always goes in the same direction. A wave differs in that the reed does not curve in the same direction but changes its curl or direction at the top and bottom of the "wave." This means we cannot work with a coil but must shape each wave.

Start by drawing two parallel chalk lines on your workboard. Make the lines as far apart as you wish the overall height of the waves to be. Next, measure off the wave peaks along one line. Then, using the same spacing, measure off the wave troughs on the second line. Make the wave troughs, or trough marks, in the center of the spaces between the wave peaks. In other words, the two series of identically spaced marks will be offset by exactly half their distances. One mark will be opposite the center of the two marks on the other line.

Drive nails into the marks. Hand-shape a wet reed so that it weaves around the nails. Fasten the ends of the reed to the workboard. Let the reed dry.

An alternate method consists of fastening a number of wood circles — similar to checkers — in a line on top of the workboard. The wet reed is then woven in and out between the guides. This is more work but makes for better results than is possible with nail guides.

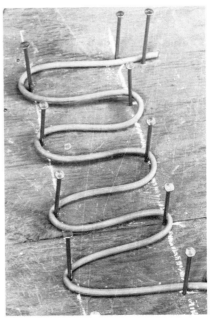

Here is one way you can put waves into reed.

Curls (spirals)   Drive two nails partway into your workboard. Space the nails just as far apart as the thickness of the reed you plan to use. Soak the reed. Slip the end of the reed between the two nails. Wrap the reed around itself in a flat spiral. Make as many turns as you wish. Make the wrapping somewhat tighter — the turns closer together — than you wish the final result to be on. The spiral will uncurl a bit when it dries. Then drive a third nail into the workboard to hold your reed end in place. Cut the excess reed.

To make a number of curls simultaneously, shape the first curl as suggested. Then drive a number of pairs of nails into the board to either side of the in-place wet reed. Now, position a number of reeds on top of the first reed. In this way you can do three or four at a time. More if you wish to duplicate the setup.

This is the way you can make a reed spiral.

Lollipops

A lollipop is a solid disk from which the stick emerges in line with its center (radius).

Start a curl as before, but take care to wrap the reed tightly upon itself. When you have made a disk the diameter you wish, drive a nail into the board to hold the last turn in place. Then bend the reed sharply away from the disk, drive one or more nails into the board to hold the reed in this position and cut it to the desired length. Then place a board or similar flat object atop the lollipop reed to hold it flat. When the reed is perfectly dry, cement the turns together.

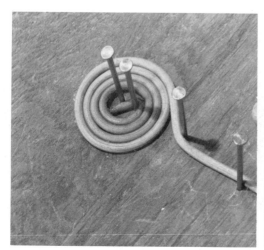

To make a reed lollipop, or closed spiral, coil wet reed as shown.

Let the reed dry. Then lock the turns together with cement.

Flowers

There are any number of ways of simulating the appearance of flowers with reed. Here are just some of them to start your imagination working:

1. Make a lollipop having a diameter of an inch or less, and a stick 5 or so inches long. Make two small curls. Place the curls alongside the lollipop stick so that the disk is between the curls. Wrap the three lengths—legs of the pop and curls together with cane. Or, depending on where the ornament will be used, nail the reeds to the piece of furniture.

2. Make an independent, closed circle of reed. Make two fairly open curls having about one or two turns and long legs. Make two smaller diameter curls having the same or fewer turns. Fasten the curls together so that the curls are paired. Large curl opposite large curls, small opposite small. Center the circle above the two large curls, and cement the reeds together. This is most easily done by placing all the reeds on a sheet of wax paper and then applying the cement to one side. When the cement is dry, turn the flower over and cement the other joints.

For greater strength wrap the joints with fine or superfine cane. Use knots and cement to tie the cane ends.

3. Start with a piece of reed two-and-a-half times longer than the desired overall length or height of the finished flower. Bend a complete, small circle in the middle of the length of reed. Bring the reed ends back together and then place the reed flat on top of your workboard. Use nails to hold the small circle almost completely closed. Then take two shorter pieces of soaked reed. Fold them in the middle, their ends back on themselves to duplicate the outlines of blades of grass. Next, place the three pieces of reed alongside each other. Position and join by one method or another.

Clefs   A clef is two curls wound in opposite directions on the ends of one piece of reed, one of the curls larger than the other. Follow the suggestions given for making single curls: Form one curl, then form the second curl on the other end of the same reed. Let it dry.

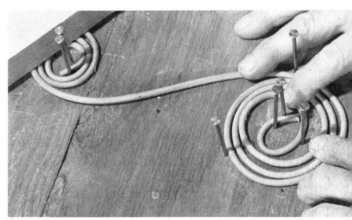

To make a clef, you wind two spirals in opposite directions on the same length of reed. Clefs, spirals, and lollipops can be joined to make flowers.

RATTAN   Rattan can be curled, circled, and waved just like reed, but needs more time and effort and in circles with far larger diameters. Whereas well-soaked ¼-inch reed can be formed into a 1-inch diameter circle or even a little less without breaking or tearing, ⅜-inch rattan—the thinnest usually available—cannot be forced into a circle much smaller than 2 inches in diameter without heating. Even with careful heating, it is difficult to go below this diameter without damaging the rattan.

The methods used for making rattan ornaments, however, remain essentially the same, except for the differences listed.

Independent circles   Soak the rattan at least 24 hours; even longer is better. Use a steel pipe or something equally strong and wrap the rattan around it. Tie the ends of the rattan in place with wire. Soak the rattan another half day while it is still on its mandrel. Remove from the water and let the rattan dry thoroughly, while it is still on its mandrel. When bone dry, remove the rattan from the mandrel. Use a hacksaw to cut the rattan into rings.

As suggested for reed circles, support the rattan ring in a vise while you drive a nail halfway into one end. Cut the nail head off.

Place some cement on the nail and rattan end. Force the other end of the rattan circle down on the nail. Press until the two ends meet. Let the cement dry.

If the two ends of the rattan circle are not aligned prior to cementing, bend the rattan until the ends are aligned. Do not depend on the cement to hold the two ends together.

MAKING INDEPENDENT CIRCLES OF RATTAN

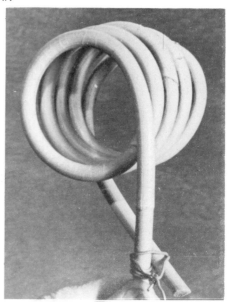

Soak the rattan 24 hours or longer. Wrap it tightly around a mandrel. A pipe will do. Soak the rattan some more.

A circle is cut from the coil. A nail is forced into one end of the reed. The other end of the rattan is forced over the end of the nail after its head has been clipped off. Then a drop of cement is placed between the ends of the rattan. The ends are forced together.

Remove the rattan and mandrel from the water. Give the rattan a good day to dry completely. Remove the rattan from the mandrel. The coil that you will end up with is shown.

This is the completed, independent circle of rattan.

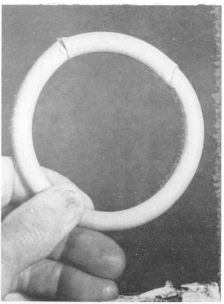

Adjoining circles Make a number of independent circles, fasten them to each other with masking tape, as previously suggested for independent circles of reed. Then fasten them to the rattan pole by one means or another. Remove the masking tape. To fasten the rings permanently to each other, drill a fine hole through two adjoining rings. Cover a nail with cement and force it through the holes. Cut off whatever nail protrudes and file smooth.

Continuous circles Follow the suggestions given for reed, but don't overlook the 24 hours of soaking necessary with rattan. Also, since the rattan is much thicker than the reed, this ornamentation has considerable thickness. For example, using ⅜-inch rattan results in an ornament having a width of ¾ inch where it turns back on itself, which is quite a bit when it is fastened to a 1-inch-diameter pole.

Waves Again the same technique suggested for reed is used, with this one difference: Whereas you can bend reed around a nail guide if you are careful, it should not be tried with rattan. Instead you need to use circular guides. You can make them by cutting off sections of a rattan pole and drilling holes through the center of each checker-shaped piece. Then screws can be used to position them on your workboard.

Split rattan Rattan can be split with a kitchen knife. Place the rattan in a vise and drive the knife down through it. Do not try to split more than a few inches at a time, and watch the split. If the knife wanders off center, angle it back. Use a hammer to drive it.

Split rattan is sometimes fastened lengthwise along one or more sides of a pole either to add interest or to hide a number of angle or parallel joints. It is also sometimes wrapped in a spiral around a pole, and sometimes in a single band. Nails are used to fasten the split rattan in place.

To split rattan, hold the rattan upright in a vise. Drive a kitchen knife down its length.

To fasten split rattan to a pole, simply nail it in place.

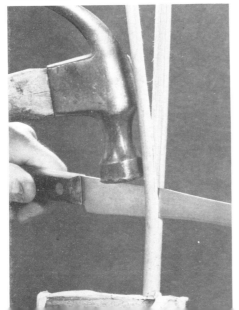

6
FINISHING AND CARE

FINISHING NEW RATTAN   Rattan is the easiest of all the materials in the world to finish. Just stand back, expand your chest, smile, and say, "Finished," and you are finished.

As probably stated more than once, rattan is covered with a hard layer of silicon, which resists weathering and wear as well, if not better, than any finish you are likely to apply to it. So, if you wish, you need do nothing to your rattan furniture when you have completed it.

However, if you want more of a shine than may be present on the poles, if you have had to sandpaper spots to remove burn marks and the like, you can cover the poles very easily with any of a number of clear finishes: enamel, varnish, or lacquer.

About paint   Before we go on to discussing the application of a clear finish, there is one point worth mentioning: Don't paint the rattan. While paint adheres as well to rattan as clear coatings, bruises and scratch marks in the clear coating are barely visible because there is no color change. But each scratch mark shows clearly on paint because each scratch reveals the pole, which is of a different color from the paint. Thus, a painted piece of furniture will look like junk after a year or two, what with highly visible scratches and color differences where the sun has rested on the paint, but a varnished or lacquered piece of furniture looks almost brand new.

In addition, should the lacquer be worn through, it is a simple matter to touch up the bare spots. This is not a simple matter with paint, because paint changes color with age; even white paint changes. This means you must have an eye as sensitive to color as Vermeer's to match the new spot of paint to the old. Or, worse yet, you have to remove all the old paint to secure a solid, one-color paint job. With clear enamel or lacquer, you sand a little to clean up the spot and spray away — a matter of minutes instead of hours.

Choice of clear finish   You can use enamel, lacquer, or varnish to finish your rattan. Enamel dries with a shine but requires several hours to dry hard. It is also sensitive to moisture in the air. On damp days drying takes much longer and if there is a film of moisture on the rattan the enamel may turn a little white. Slow drying not only delays your work, but the longer the coating remains soft and sticky, the greater the chance that wandering dust will settle and leave marks.

There are two types of lacquers available today. One dries flat, which means it has no shine or gloss. The other does have a gloss when dry. Both dry rapidly. If you plan to apply a second coat, it is best to let 48 hours pass before you do so, using either type of lacquer.

Varnish can also be used, but the spray cans marked "varnish" today usually contain clear polyurethane, a type of plastic coating. Polyurethane differs from lacquer in that it dries better in moist air than dry, and it is best not to wait too long before applying a second coat. It too is available in matt or gloss finish. See the can for directions.

Preparation
Rub the rattan lightly with fine steel wool or #400 sandpaper. This is done to give the surface "tooth," which simply means a surface that the coating can adhere to. The dust or whatever that is produced by rubbing should be carefully removed or it will roughen the finish.

Prepare a room or area for spraying by spreading a solid layer of newspapers on the floor to cover an area approximately 10 feet by 10 feet. Indoors, vacuum the balance of the room. Outdoors, wet the earth or grass or driveway around the paper so that there is little possibility of dust being blown onto the rattan you are going to finish. For simplicity, the rattan to be finished will be called the work piece.

Do not work if the temperature goes below 70 degrees F. It is better if it is higher. Eighty degrees or so is ideal.

Application method
Although you may think you will save considerable money when you have a lot of furniture to finish if you use a brush instead of a spray can, don't use a brush. Not only is a brush much slower and far more tedious, it is very difficult to do a good job with a brush. It is easy with a spray can (or powered sprayer).

Application
Start by turning the work piece upside down, legs up in the air. Hold the can about 8 inches from the work piece and off to one side. Push the button down, taking care to keep your thumb clear. Swing the can and the emerging spray all the way along the work piece. Release the button only after your spray is beyond the work piece.

Never start the spray directly on the work piece. Never stop the spray directly on the work piece. Never swing the spray back and forth on the work piece, but *always* go past the work piece before returning the spray in the other direction.

If you point the can at the work piece and then push the button, you will have a blob of enamel or what have you where you start. If you reverse yourself in the middle of a swing, you get the same blob. Stopping and starting the spray beyond the work piece may "waste" enamel, but it is the only way to get a good job.

Vary the distance between the can and the work piece in order to lay down a "wet" coating. But not so much enamel that it runs. On the other hand, if the coating on the work piece does not look wet as it strikes, you are holding the can too far away.

Do not attempt to get spray into the cracks and crevices. The spray will not enter; all that will happen is that you will pile up the enamel and produce a run.

Be certain to coat the ends of the poles and to permit sufficient time to pass for the spray coating to dry hard before you turn the work piece right side up and continue your work.

Clear the nozzle of the can before putting it down for more than a minute. If you don't, it will clog up and you will not be able to use the balance of the liquid in the can Simply invert the can, press the button, and hold it until no more liquid emerges; just air.

FINISHING OLD RATTAN

Rattan furniture that has been in use for any length of time is always covered with a fine film of oil. This interferes with the adhesion of the enamel or lacquer or whatever you may choose to use. So the first step to finishing or refinishing old rattan consists of cleaning it.

Slop some clear, denatured alcohol on a clean dry cloth and wipe the entire piece of furniture down. Take special care with the arm rests, because that is where body oils are most likely to accumulate. If there are thick encrustations of old enamel, use paint remover to remove it. Then follow the instructions for finishing new rattan. Incidentally, paint remover should be removed with alcohol.

FINISHING CANE

Follow the suggestions given for finishing new and old rattan, but take care not to apply a thick coating to the cane. Do not coat the underside of the cane. Let it be. There is no need for a protective coating here.

FINISHING REED

Reed can be finished with a clear coating, as suggested for rattan and cane. But since reed is highly absorbent, you must make certain it is truly bone dry before spraying it.

Reed also takes paint very well, but one doesn't usually paint reed when it is attached to varnished rattan.

SHELLAC

Shellac is useful for floors and as a primary coating on table tops prior to varnish. But shellac should never be used on contact furniture. With heat—even no more than body heat—shellac becomes soft and sticky. I'm certain no one would care to sit on a shellac-covered chair on a warm day.

FINISHING SPLINT

Splint made from hardwood can be treated exactly like rattan. However, since it is porous, it does not need to be given a rubdown with steel wool or sandpaper prior to spraying.

Splint made from reed is really nothing more than flat, wide reed and can be treated as such.

CARE

Rattan, reed, cane, splint, and the rest are tough and are not damaged by an occasional shower. But no rattan should be turned out to pasture each summer and forgotten. The sun will bleach the color out, the cane will become overly dry, and rot will creep up its legs. By the same token rattan furniture should not be stored in a damp cellar; it will rot.

On the other hand, rattan furniture, especially the cane, does need a little moisture. Should the cane become too dry, you will notice that it loosens. Therefore if the furniture is not where moisture can reach it naturally—if you live in Arizona, Utah, or Israel, where the air is always very dry—this writer suggests you hose the rattan down once or twice a year. Running water will get the dust out of the cracks and bring the cane's moisture content back to normal.

Otherwise, rattan furniture needs no more than an occasional dusting. Furniture polish and wax are normally never used.

CLEANING   All the natural fibers and woods can be hosed down without any problem or question with the exception of sea grass. Neither this fiber nor the "fiber" made of twisted Kraft paper should be cleaned with more than a damp cloth and a little soap. Soaking will loosen sea grass and the paper will disintegrate.

If hosing alone is insufficient, use a small brush and some mild soap to get the job done. Follow with a cool water rinse.

Paint removal   Years ago it was customary to paint the wicker every spring. In time the furniture became more paint than wicker. The only practical way to remove all the paint from such pieces is to have a professional "stripper" do the job. He places the piece in a large tank and hoses it down with a paint remover. He can bring the piece down to the bare wood or reed. You can't, without spending an inordinate amount of time and money on paint remover.

Bleaching   With the paint or varnish removed, you can lighten the color of the wicker by using a mild bleach. Try a little Clorox or similar laundry bleach on a hidden corner. If that works, do the entire piece, taking care to apply the bleach to the entire piece of furniture at one time—a minute or so pause doesn't matter. Wait until the bleach does the job, but not more than 30 minutes or so. Then remove the bleach with a hose. If bleach won't give you the results you want, it may be that the wicker is permanently stained or requires a stronger bleach. Try a commercial wood bleach—the two-solution bleach is the strongest—but use great care, since you can not only burn yourself, but you can bring the wood or wicker to an unsightly dead white in a short time. Note too that bleach weakens the surface of wicker and reed.

7
DESIGNING RATTAN FURNITURE

If you are reading this book, you are probably the kind of person who enjoys making things. If you are, you will enjoy designing just as much, if not more. If you believe designing rattan furniture is difficult and beyond you, since you have never designed any furniture, much less rattan furniture, you are wrong. It is easy.

Not only is the design of rattan furniture easy, it is also necessary. No single book could possibly contain all the different types, styles, and construction methods utilized and possible in the making of rattan furniture. The projects described in the following pages cannot, by any stretch of the imagination, satisfy the needs and desires of all the readers of this book.

If you simply make the pieces suggested, you will have utilized very little of what this book has to offer. But if you apply your imagination to all the technical construction data provided, there is no limit to what you can do with rattan. You can literally make any piece of rattan furniture you can imagine or that you see.

Design is not discovery or even invention. Design is the act of assembling and arranging known components. In our case, rattan, cane, reed, etc., into known shapes — chairs, tables, beds, etc.

Each shape, each chair, table, bed, what have you, is a known quantity. Its dimensions are known. For example, dining and kitchen tabletops are usually 30 inches above the floor. Chair seats are usually 18 inches above the floor.

The minimum number of parts each shape must have to be stable and useful is also known. For example, a chair or table must have three legs at a minimum or it will tip over. Most have four, but you can have five or six or more.

Rattan furniture is especially easy to design. It is open. It is constructed of poles, much like Tinker Toys. By comparison, standard wood furniture is very difficult to design (and construct). You work with solid materials; the joints are complicated, difficult, and must be carefully considered in the overall design. You also have to know board dimensions, types of wood, different joints, hardware, finishes, and so on. Rattan utilizes only a few different joints.

BUILDING A MODEL   It is difficult to envision standard, solid wood furniture even after the design has been carefully drawn to scale. A drawing doesn't provide a sense of mass. Even photographs really fail in this respect. You don't really know how a standard piece of furniture will look in your home from a photograph or drawing alone. A three-dimensional scale model would of course be of immeasurable help; but making an accurate model of a piece of furniture is a time-consuming job.

Not so with rattan. You can easily and quickly make a scale model of your design by using reed. Simply follow the procedures suggested for making reed ornaments. Soak the reed, bend and hold it to the desired shape with nails or pins until it dries. Then cement the pieces together.

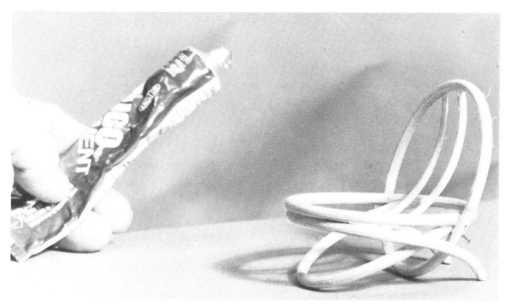

A miniature model of a chair made with reed, pins, and cement. While this is a very interesting and attractive design, it is difficult to construct because of the many curves utilized.

BASIC DIMENSIONS   The accompanying drawings illustrate the major basic dimensions utilized for modern furniture. The most important are those having to do with heights of seats and table; bed widths and lengths.

If you make a chair either too high or too low, it will be uncomfortable for the average person. The same goes for tabletops at which some one will sit. If you err in designing a bed, you may not be able to find a standard mattress that will fit it.

Most other dimensions can be varied somewhat. For example, coffee table heights are not critical. Widths and lengths of dining room tables are only important in relation to the table cloths or pad you plan to use with them.

Should you be uncertain about any dimension, stop and measure a similar piece of furniture made by other means. Should you be planning to use pads and the like, measure them before you proceed.

CONVENTIONAL FURNITURE DIMENSIONS

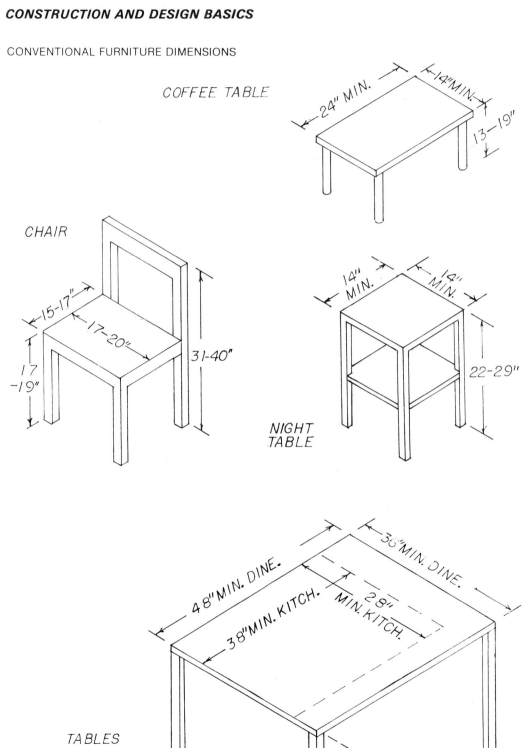

COFFEE TABLE

24" MIN.

14" MIN.

13–19"

CHAIR

15–17"

17–20"

31–40"

17 –19"

14" MIN.

14" MIN.

22–29"

NIGHT TABLE

36" MIN. DINE.

48" MIN. DINE.

38" MIN. KITCH.

28" MIN. KITCH.

29–30"

TABLES

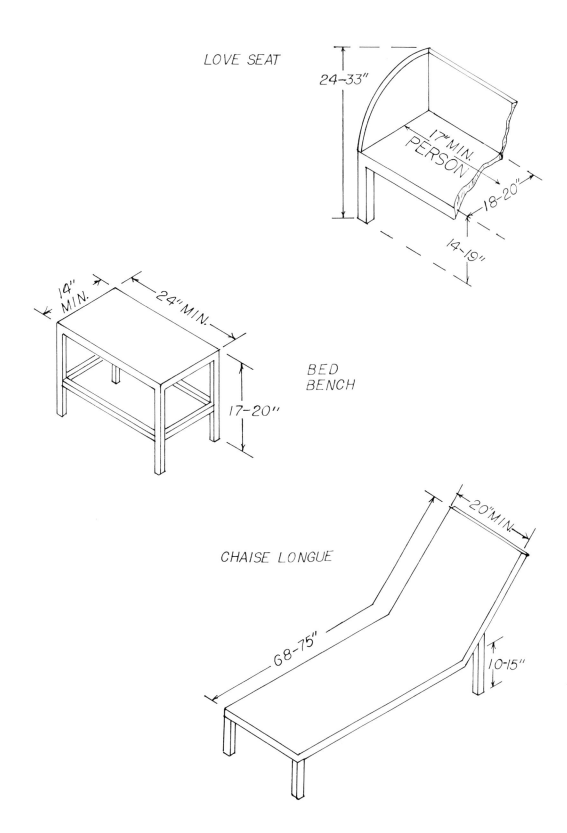

LOVE SEAT

24–33"

17" MIN.
PERSON

18–20"

14–19"

14" MIN.

24" MIN.

BED
BENCH

17–20"

CHAISE LONGUE

20" MIN.

68–75"

10–15"

Supporting surfaces

Rattan furniture utilizes four types or kinds of supporting surfaces: glass, as for a tabletop; wood; woven material (cane reed, etc.); and rattan.

When you design for any of these materials, you must allow for their thickness and/or for what will go on top. For example, if you are going to use a ¾-inch plywood panel for the top of a table, the ¾ inch must be added when planning the table's height.

Woven materials such as cane, reed, splint, and their like, can be used directly as supporting surfaces. That is to say, you can sit directly on woven cane or reed or splint. Thus the upper surfaces of these materials may be the top surface of a chair or bench.

While rattan is used as a supporting surface—it can be woven or the pieces placed so closely to one another the rattan acts as a mat—it is almost never used alone. Rattan is virtually always topped by a cushion or sheet of glass. Therefore, when you plan to place a cushion or sheet of glass, plastic, or wood on top of a supporting surface, you must include the thickness of the material in your calculation of overall height—not just the height of the supporting surface by itself.

In addition, you must include the nature of the material you are going to use. Wood or glass does not flatten under load, but cushions do. Obviously, you cannot determine an exact figure, but you can estimate. For example, a firm cushion 4 inches thick will probably be compressed to a thickness of 3 inches when sat on. Thus to make a chair seat 18 inches high, using this cushion, you need a supporting surface 15 inches high. With the cushion alone the top of the chair seat is 19 inches above the ground. In use the chair's seat sinks to the desired 18 inches.

Building to the component, not the other way around

Assuming you plan to use tie-on cushions, pads, glass, or whatever, start your design by securing the exact measurements of these components. Don't guess or work from an advertisement. If you do, you may find the item has been sold out by the time you get there, or the published figure, given as standard, has been rounded off or is in error. The "standard" 25-inch cushion measures out to no more than 23¼ inches, and so on.

The best and least dangerous method is to purchase the components before you start designing, or at least to have them on hand before you begin cutting and bending rattan. Doing this, you can't miss. You won't find yourself paying two and three times more to have a sheet of plate glass cut to size, when a precut and polished sheet, costing much less, doesn't fit your already completed table.

And, by working from the component, you need not limit yourself to standard-size material. You can utilize odd-size components and slightly used components that are no longer of a common or standard size. Tremendous savings can be secured this way.

Just remember, it is easy enough to vary dimensions before you build; almost impossible afterward.

LOADING   *Loading* is the technical term for the weight, or load, to be carried by a beam or what have you. To us it means simply deciding on how thick a pole must be to do its job without bending too much. In many instances the choice of pole diameter will be obvious. You just know by feel that a pole will or will not be able to do the necessary job. In other instances, you can simply duplicate what is suggested in this book or what you see elsewhere.

If you are uncertain and can find no similar piece of rattan construction, try supporting the pole as you plan to, say on two boxes, and pushing down in its middle. Or if you want to estimate the load a short length of pole can take, clamp one end in a vise and push or pull on its other end.

A long horizontal pole can be strengthened by using short vertical support poles along its length. Long poles can also be strengthened by doubling them. Fasten two side by side with screws and cane wrappings. Short and long poles can be firmed up by using braces. There are many ways of making thin poles carry a heavy load. You don't need automatically to go to a thick pole when a thin pole seems inadequate.

BENDS, CURLS, AND CURVES   A straight line is still the shortest distance between two points. If you choose to traverse the distance with a curve or curl, you will need that much longer a piece of rattan. Lots of curves and curls on a piece of rattan furniture will greatly increase the quantity of rattan you will need to construct it.

A straight piece of rattan is quickly measured and cut to size. A curved piece of rattan requires planning and time.

But beauty lies in the eye of the beholder. So as the designer, you must decide how many bends and curves your furniture will include, if any. Just refer to the table listing the minimum circle diameters to which poles of various thicknesses can be bent without damage. Make certain your plan doesn't call for an impossibly tight bend. Bear in mind that the more shallow the curve or bend, the easier it is to make.

Stay away from complex bends or multiple bends on a single pole. It is far easier to make one bend on each of two poles than two bends on one pole. It is also very difficult to make bends accurately in two directions or planes on a single pole. If the pole is to be bent up and down, for example, don't plan on also bending it sideways; you will have lots of trouble holding these curves to your desired shape and size.

Also think about composite bends. Instead of using one thick pole, for example, to make a circle or curve, think about the possibility of using two thin poles side by side.

POLE LENGTH   In all your planning you must keep in mind the length of the poles you will use. If you are just going to mail-order a few poles, you will be limited to poles under 6 feet in length because of parcel post restrictions. If you purchase a sufficient number of poles to make a truck shipment practical (this need by no means be a full truckload), you can count on poles of 8 to 10 feet in length. Rattan of ¼ inch or less in diameter can be rolled into coils and easily shipped by parcel post.

Short poles are not as limiting as you may at first imagine. Lots can be done with short poles. Where they must be longer, they can be spliced. Another method you can use to secure long thick poles is to nail, glue, and wrap two or three thin poles into a bundle. To bend such composite poles, bend each thin pole separately and then bundle them.

DESIGNING

Now, finally, after beating around the bush, we come to the actual practice of designing. Sorry about that, but there was no other way to get here. Unless you know, understand, and appreciate all the factors discussed, what follows will be of little practical value to you:

Freehand sketch

Start by sketching your design on a sheet of paper. Then redraw it and redraw it again and again until you have what you like. Then apply all the criteria previously discussed. See that you meet all the requirements. Decide whether or not you want all the curves; whether or not the curves and bends are too complex, or too tight, or otherwise impractical.

Consider the joints you are going to use. Consider the number of pieces of rattan you will need. Is there any way of reducing the rattan without weakening the structure, reducing its charm? Change your design if necessary.

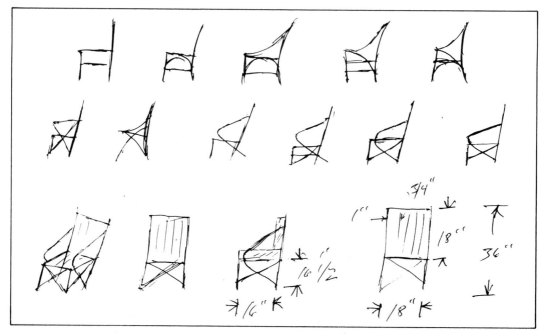

How a chair design can be developed through a series of rough sketches. Final design, bottom right, was considered acceptable because it was practical, had only two bends, and looked good. During actual construction, it may be found necessary to add some braces on the bottoms of the legs. But this can be put off until the chair is actually constructed.

Determine next the thickness and lengths of the poles you will need. Make certain you can secure poles this long. Think about cutting the poles. How can you cut them so as to end up with the least number of short pieces, which are generally waste because they cannot be used?

If you are going to splice, position your splice so that it will not be within a bend and, if possible, so it will be out of sight.

If there are to be bends and curves, try to keep them similar so that you can use the same workboard drawing and guide for all or most of them.

Scale of drawing

Next draw your design to scale on graph paper, taking great care to be as accurate as possible. Show the side, front, top, and back views — more if necessary. This is necessary because we often unconsciously fudge when we sketch. Put the dimensions on the drawings.

Make up a list of material, with all necessary dimensions. Remember, if you plan on mortise joints, you have to allow for the length of the tenons. If you are going to chamfer the pole ends on T joints before fastening them, you also have to allow for the depth of the curve you will make.

Making a model

If you are uncertain as to how your design will look full size, make a scale model of reed. This takes a little time, but it will enable you to secure a much more realistic preview of what you are going to construct than is possible from a mechanical drawing, or even an isometric drawing.

8
CONSTRUCTION TIPS

WHEN TO START
If you are enthused about making your own rattan furniture, it is only natural that you will be anxious to begin as soon as you have some of the materials on hand. Don't.

Your eagerness is commendable, but let caution temper your enthusiasm. Do not start construction until you have all the necessary materials on hand, including glass tops and cushions if you are going to use them. Even large supply houses have the troublesome problem of running out of supplies now and again. Very often manufacturers of cushions, glass panels, and the like change dimensions without forewarning. So wait until you have everything necessary before you start to build your furniture. And do not start until you have drawn your project to scale — or used the included drawings — and have made up a parts list including all the necessary dimensions for the parts.

SEPARATING YOUR STOCK
If you purchase your rattan poles by the bundle — and this is the way you should buy poles because the cost is a fraction of what you will pay by the individual, short pole, even with the added-on cost of trucking — you will do well to examine and separate the poles in each bundle before you start work. Spread them out on the floor and examine each of them.

Most often, each bundle will contain a variety of pole diameters within the specified size. For example, if you order a bundle of 1-inch poles, you will find some poles that barely make the inch requirement and some poles that go to 1¼ inches. You will find some poles are almost straight, while other poles are quite curved. Some poles will be almost perfectly free of growth marks and other defects; other poles will speckled, spotted, and bumpy.

Each pole is especially suited to some particular portion of rattan furniture construction. The curved poles are best for bent parts — the curve is already in the wood. The spotted poles may be used for less visible sections of the furniture, the thicker poles for the parts that need the additional strength.

In this way you can get a lot more out of the bundle than if you just took the poles as they came to hand.

Incidentally, though the surface of the rattan is very tough and hard, it is still inadvisable to drag or push poles across a wood or concrete floor. They will still be somewhat damaged. So treat them with care.

Planning your cutting
You have your material. Now, with dimensions and parts list in hand, mark off your rattan cuts, but do not cut the poles. Instead, review your marks and see whether or not you can shift cuts from one pole to another so as to eliminate the short ends, or at least reduce their number.

The foregoing may sound silly, but your poles will never be of equal length. Lengths may vary as much as a foot or more from pole to pole. It is a pity to cut two 7-foot 6-inch poles to get two 4-foot lengths when you may have an 8-foot pole on hand.

When you have marked all the required cuts—you can do this with masking tape and pencil—put the poles aside. It is still not time to cut any of them.

MAKING FULL-SIZE DRAWINGS If you are going to use nothing but straight pieces of rattan, you can skip this. But if you are going to include bent or curved pieces in your design, the next step consists of laying out the desired curves full scale on your workboard. Cut guides from scrap lumber and position them as necessary. Mark the desired ends of the piece or pieces to be bent on the workboard.

See whether or not you have to repeat any of the bends. Perhaps a slight change in design will allow you to build your furniture with, let us say, four identically bent pieces of rattan in place of four slightly differently curved pieces. Since it is much easier to repeat a bend than to make a different one, changing designs when possible to use repeat bends reduces the labor involved in construction.

BENDING Note that not a word has been said about cutting any of the poles as yet. Unless you have considerable experience—and even then it is not too good a practice—do not cut any pole until you have shaped it. (The uncut end also provides additional leverage when bending.)

Bending together You will find it easier if you make all the necessary bends first rather than bend one pole, cut it and then bend another. With all the uncut and bent pieces in hand you can often select a compromise shape or bend, and correct or alter the others by cold bending them a little. Long and uncut, the poles are easier to handle.

It is next to impossible to make each bend or curve exactly as designed. Therefore, you will have to make slight adjustments and variations in the furniture you construct. If you do not accept these minor variations—which are hardly ever noticeable in the finished piece of furniture—you will find yourself bending forever.

To accommodate these variations, put off cutting until you are certain you have the *shape you can use*. Then when you are certain, cut away as necessary.

TRIAL ASSEMBLY You may find it helpful to assemble the pieces of your furniture temporarily before you join them permanently. This can be done with masking tape, string, and even soft wire.

Sometimes the temporarily assembled piece will look different than it did in your drawing and different even from the model you may have constructed.

In some cases you will be stuck with what you have wrought. In others you will be able to change the appearance by moving the various parts a little — for example, change the angle of the legs or back of a chair; change the pivot point of a chair on rockers; lower or even raise a chaise. Sometimes just moving a brace or altering its shape can change the appearance of an entire piece of furniture.

If you've planned carefully and avoided jumping into a project before the placement of all the elements has been carefully calculated, you will be unlikely to have to contend with more than minor alterations to get a satisfactory piece of furniture. On a rare occasion you may find that your calculations didn't provide you with plans for a piece that you're comfortable with. And you may not discover that until you try assembling it. Well, if you haven't immediately joined the pieces permanently, you can at least spare yourself that work, and in many cases you can use the pieces of rattan to make other things. Once you join the parts ''permanently,'' you also have the labor of disassembly and the waste of pieces with holes, tapered ends, etc. The real secret to saving unnecessary work lies in the advance conceptualization and planning.

And a final point: Temporary fastening can be of great help in positioning and making permanent joints. For example, you may want to position a chair rung perfectly horizontally. You can do this by measuring up from the chair leg bottoms. But, in some instances you will have to alter chair leg length in order to make the chair perfectly upright. When the rung is already in place and horizontal and you later alter a leg, the result will be a rung that is no longer exactly horizontal.

Temporary fastening will also hold parts together for you so that you can make the necessary holes for screws and start nails much more easily than if you have to handhold the parts in position.

JIGS   A jig is a device that holds parts in proper relation so that they can be permanently joined.

When you are making a number of identical pieces of furniture — or anything else for that matter — it pays to make a complete jig so that you can simply fit the pieces in place and fasten them.

While such a jig is very neat and handy, it is impractical for making a single piece of furniture. However, even a partial jig can be of great help. For example, you are assembling a table or chair or anything else having a number of legs which must be held in alignment. You can start by marking the position of each leg on your workboard and using the marks to locate the legs. Then, to keep the legs from moving around you can position blocks of wood around the leg ends and nail the blocks to the workboard.

Another example would be the use of a small board nailed in a vertical position alongside, let us say, a table. By just holding one side of the table against the board, which acts as a try square, you know your table and its legs are vertical.

These two suggestions do not by any means cover all the possibilities, but they should set you thinking as to how you can ease construction and assembly and at the same time improve the final product.

NAILING

You will find it very difficult to drive home even the smallest nail unless you place the rattan on some solid support. This can be a bench or chair. If the shape of the piece you are working on precludes placing it on a chair—let us say you are nailing to a vertical leg—hold a second hammer behind the leg, or even a brick or stone. If you don't, the leg will vibrate and you will bend the nail.

PRECISION

If you come to the making of rattan furniture from a machine shop or even after having some cabinetmaking experience, you may find it difficult to accept the absence of precision in the making of rattan furniture. The precision or accuracy of cabinetry or even carpentry is impossible in rattan work; or at least highly impractical.

You start with poles that are tapered. Even though the palm tree may have changed diameter only a few inches in several hundred feet of length, you will find that the difference in the diameter of the two ends of even a short pole is fairly obvious. You don't need to measure to find the thinnest end of a rattan pole. When you go to bend any pole, by any method you will find a marked difference in bending response between pole ends. The thinner section bends much more easily than the thicker. Because of this it is impossible simply to bring the two ends of a pole together and get a perfect arc. The result will always be a varying curve. To make it into a perfect arc you have to *bend* the pole to your requirements.

In addition, you will find that the rattan does not bend as easily at the joints as it does between the joints. If you are a purist and examine any piece of bent rattan you will find it to be a series of curves separated by straight sections. The straight sections are where the joints are.

You will also find that very few, if any, rattan poles are perfectly straight. They all have some sort of natural bend or bends. If you attempt to take the very last vestige of these bends out of the poles, you will find yourself putting other small bends in the poles.

Art, not anarchy

To craftsmen schooled in the disciplines of the machine shop, cabinetmaking shop, or even carpentry shops, where an open space of more than $\frac{1}{64}$ inch is a sloppy joint (in machining, $\frac{1}{5000}$ inch is a sloppy joint), rattan furniture may seem hopelessly crooked and crude. This is true. Rattan furniture *is* crooked and uneven and crude. But *this is rattan*. This is the nature of the material and the nature of its construction. And this is the charm and beauty of rattan. It is informal, rustic, and natural. It is put together on a functional basis.

Try to make all your joints tight and square, try to keep all the vertical parts as vertical as you can. But don't waste time and temper trying for perfection. It is almost impossible and certainly unnecessary. If the furniture you make looks good, it is good. Don't put a rule and try square to the finished product. It is unnecessary.

A WORD ABOUT THE PROJECTS AND THE WORK   Once you have started building rattan furniture, you will discover that the work is easy, pleasant, satisfying, and without a doubt the most practical and economical way of building "real" furniture for your home, as gifts, and even as a secondary source of income.

The projects detailed in this book and the furniture you yourself can design are beautiful, strong, light, and long-lasting. They are equal to anything you can purchase in the shops. They will make beautiful, permanent additions to your home, additions you will be proud of.

Even if you have never constructed anything of wood before, you will not fail with rattan. It is the nature of the material. It lends itself to what may be termed freehand construction. Rattan furniture is supposed to look "native," so any little vagaries in design or construction are normal and expected.

The projects given in Part Two have been selected on the basis of simplicity, material economy, and construction ease. They may appear to be difficult, but they are not. Even a beginning craftsman or craftswoman will have no trouble constructing them in a reasonable amount of time.

None of the dimensions are sacrosanct; but don't go to thicker or thinner poles without due thought. Pole diameters have been selected on the basis of a three-way compromise between necessary stiffness, bending needs, and cost. Remember, the thicker poles cost more. If you go to a heavier pole, you may not be able to bend it as required. If you go to a thinner pole, you may find the completed piece of furniture springy and wobbly. (It is doubtful, however, that the furniture will break under load just because you used a slightly thinner pole.)

Furniture size is based on custom, body requirements, and pleasing design. There is no reason why you cannot change any design any way you wish, just as long as you satisfy human requirements: seat height, table height, etc.

Follow the construction step sequences suggested. Doing so should make construction simpler and easier. Don't skip on the jigs and guides. Don't make any joint permanent until you are certain it is correct. Very often, when several parts of the furniture you are constructing are not exactly the way you wanted them to be, a slight shifting of joints can bring everything square and shipshape again. Remember, a few holes mean nothing in the final appearance of the furniture. You can always plug them with a little putty.

If you do encounter difficulty, it will probably be in the bending of the thicker pieces of rattan. In such cases use a length of pipe slipped over the end of the pole to give you added leverage. Remember, the pole doesn't soften much with heat. You have to bend it first, then apply the heat so that it remains bent.

Also, beware of letting go of the pole when you have removed the torch. Not only should you hold the pole until it has cooled down, which will help it retain its bend; thick poles have considerable spring. If you let it go, it may fly up and hurt you.

As you work, you will quickly gain skill and confidence. You will be better able to judge the necessary overbending by eye. You'll be bending in minutes poles that previously may have taken you a half hour. You will pick up and develop little short cuts and techniques that will expedite and ease the work. You will develop a system and a better understanding of the materials and the methods.

With a little experience, you will be able to do the smaller projects in a few hours. The largest and most complicated pieces of furniture should not take you more than a day or two.

The dimensions and parts lists provided are based on specific cushions, pieces of glass, and similar furniture parts. If you use different-size cushions and pieces of glass, you must remember to alter all the associated dimensions accordingly.

Figures that read, for example, ½-¾ inch simply mean that a pole with a diameter of ½ inch to ¾ inch is recommended. Figures that read, for example, 1 + inch mean that a pole 1 inch thick or thicker may be used.

Part Two

Rattan Construction Projects

9
COFFEE TABLE (DESIGN ONE)

PARTS LIST		
	Glass top	$\frac{5}{16}$-inch plate, 30 or so inches in diameter
	Legs	5 or more pieces 1$\frac{1}{4}$-inch rattan pole, 16 inches long
	Hoops	2 pieces $\frac{5}{8}$ + -inch rattan pole, 75 inches long
	Binding cane	26 feet
	Nails	Handful 4-penny finishing

The coffee table illustrated is one of the easiest and simplest pieces of rattan furniture you can build. Though its design is more or less modern, it will fit in well with many other types and styles of furniture.

There is no hot bending. The circles or hoops are formed by simply pulling and pushing the rattan pole into shape. The vertical pieces or legs are straight, or as straight as any natural pieces of rattan ever are. All the joints are glued and nailed. The splices are hidden by wrappings, so they do not have to be visually perfect or near perfect.

Tabletop height and the size of the glass top are arbitrary. Generally coffee tables are 17 inches high. This one is 16 inches high — that is the way the poles on hand worked out. Hoop diameters are 22 inches and 21½ inches. This was done to give the legs a slight inward tilt toward the top, which makes the table more attractive.

There are five legs. More might provide a more interesting appearance. Fewer would definitely result in a much weaker table. It wouldn't fall down, but it would be springy and wobbly.

Leg diameter is 1+ inches. One inch is sufficient, if you do not have thicker poles, but do not go to less than 1-inch legs if you are not going to use more than five legs. Again, the result will be a wobbly table.

The hoops are made of $\frac{5}{8}$-inch poles. Thicker hoops will produce greater table rigidity but may require wet heat for bending. Five-eighths of an inch is just about as thick as you can go on a circle of this diameter without the need of wet heat.

The glass top is 30 inches across and $\frac{5}{8}$-inch thick. Slightly thinner glass is satisfactory, but don't go to anything less than ¼-inch plate. It is too weak. It may break at the drop of a tea cup.

MAKING THE HOOPS   Start by measuring the diameter of the glass top you are going to use. Anything from 20 to 35 inches will do, but smaller or larger circles of glass will prove awkward.

Make the upper hoop roughly two-thirds the diameter of the glass. In this case, a 75-inch piece of ⅝-inch rattan on hand bent neatly into a 22-inch hoop with 5 inches of overlap, so that was used.

The rattan will not quietly roll itself up into a circle on demand. You have to force it to do this. The easy way is to form it into a large loop, then reduce the diameter of the hoop by sliding one end of the pole over the other. Keep doing this until you have a circle much smaller than the one you want. The when you release it, it may spring out to a diameter close to what you need. If the pole keeps springing out to a large loop when you let go, use rope or tape to hold it in a small hoop form. Then submerge the rattan beneath water for a day. When you release the water-soaked pole, it will have lost much of its spring.

To make certain your hoops are both circular and of the desired diameter, draw a circle of the desired diameter on your workboard. You can do this with chalk, a nail, and some string. Use the nail as the center point, and the string as the leg of the compass. Then you can readily check circularity and size by just placing the hoop over the chalk circle.

When you have bent the rattan into the desired circle, join its ends with a long splice, using cement or glue and some 1¼-inch #16 wire brads. Do not use more than four brads — you may split the pole ends — and make the splice at least 4 inches long. If the brad points protrude, file them off. If you try to bend them over, you may split the pole ends. Give the cement or glue a chance to set before you do anything else to the hoops.

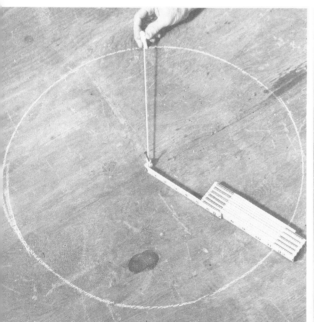

Draw the circles that will serve as a guide for the hoops. To make one hoop smaller than the other, adjust it to fit within the circle.

The ends of the hoops are being nailed together in a splice. Then the hoop will be bent a little to make it conform to the circle.

MAKING THE LEGS Measure the rattan poles you have on hand and divide the poles into five or more pieces of identical length. As previously stated, the top of the coffee table does not have to be any particular height—any height will do so long as it serves your purpose. Some modern coffee tables are only 13 inches above the floor.

With the legs cut to size and on hand, construct a jig on your workboard, consisting of two pieces of wood. Any scrap lumber having straight sides will do. If you have no scrap lumber, purchase some 1 × 2 furring strips. They will do fine and are the cheapest lumber you can buy.

With the aid of a square, position the two pieces of wood, each about 2 feet long, into a right angle. Nail the strips to the workboard; a couple of nails driven only partly into the workboard will do.

Now, align the legs, side by side, using the jig to hold their ends in line and the legs vertical to their ends. All this may appear to be just a bother, but it is necessary.

If we were dealing with dowels, which are perfectly straight bars of wood, we could measure up from any end and be reasonably certain of accuracy. But since rattan is usually slightly curved or bent, we cannot measure in from the ends. Instead we align the poles—in this case legs—more or less parallel with one another with the aid of the jig. Then we measure up from the jig and draw a line across the legs.

No matter how much of a curve there may be in each leg, when the legs are positioned reasonably vertically, that line will be parallel with the floor.

On short pieces inaccuracy might not be noticeable, but on a long piece of rattan the error would be obvious. You might, for example, measure 5 feet up the length of a crooked pole. When you stand the pole up in a vertical position, the mark could easily be an inch or more less than 5 feet above the floor. The amount of error would depend on the curve or curves in the pole and its length.

Getting back to our coffee table legs, measure 4 inches up from the lower end of the leg touching the jig. Mark this on the jig. Then measure down 4 inches from the end of the same leg. Mark this also on the jig. Then, with the aid of a square, carry these two marks across the five, reasonably parallel legs.

Once the lines are drawn, use a coarse round file, a round Surform file, or even coarse sandpaper wrapped around a piece of rattan to cut a semicircular groove, or chamfer, across each leg. Each groove is to be just as deep as half the thickness of the hoop that is to fit into the groove. You will find a short piece of rattan of the same diameter as the hoop material very helpful as a means of quickly checking the grooves.

Take care to hold the groove straight across the leg and keep it as close to the diameter of the hoop rattan as possible. You want a snug fit here. File and work slowly. Whether you find it easier to groove all the legs simultaneously or one at a time is something you will have to decide for yourself. The grooves are, of course, centered on the lines you have drawn on the legs.

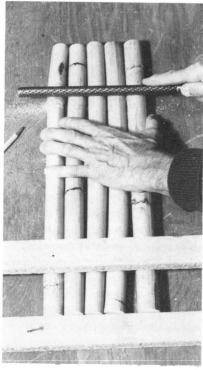

The five legs have been marked. The grooves are being cut across them. At first it was easier to groove them all together. When the goove became deeper, the poles were grooved individually.

The hoop is nailed within a groove on a leg. The nail is not driven home at this time so that corrections can be made if needed.

ASSEMBLY

With the legs cut and chamfered, divide the hoops into five equal parts with pencil marks. Place one leg on a bench or chair top. Place one hoop in a groove, the pencil mark centered over the center of the leg. Drive a 4-penny finishing nail partway through the hoop and into the leg. The leg needs support while you nail.

Next nail the four other legs to the same hoop. Then nail the legs to the second hoop. If you have made the two hoops slightly different in size—by design or accident—don't worry about which hoop you nail in place first; this table base can be used either side up.

Checking for accuracy

At this juncture you have two hoops lightly nailed to five or more legs. The entire assembly is wobbly and shaky. Lift it gently and stand it on a smooth and level floor. Then with a try square or your trusty eye alone, examine each leg to see that it is reasonably vertical and that it is in reasonably good alignment with its neighbors. If you want the legs to be vertical from all sides and the leg slants outward a bit at the top, try cutting the lower groove a little deeper. If the legs are crooked, remove the nails and renail the hoops to the legs. Do this one leg at a time.

Meanwhile, keep in mind that old rattan craftsman saying, "If it looks good, it is good."

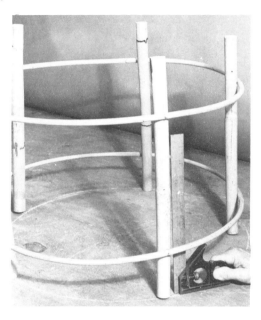

The hoops have been nailed to the legs. Now they are checked for verticalness.

Final assembly
When you are satisfied that the legs are as perfectly aligned as they will ever be, pull the hoops clear of the grooves by a fraction of an inch. Force cement or glue between the hoop and legs. Push the hoops back into their joints. Drive the nail snug. Do not overdrive it; you may split the rattan. Give the cement or glue lots of time to set.

WRAPPING
.When the cement or glue is hard, it is time to wrap the joints. You will need approximately 20 feet of binding cane for each hoop. It is not necessary to work with a single strand of cane on each hoop. You can cut it into shorter pieces if you wish.

Setting up a pattern
You can wrap each joint as you wish when you come to it, but if you want them to look reasonably alike, it is best to set up a pattern — any pattern — and keep repeating it at each joint. Just remember, the purpose of the wrapping in this case is twofold: to hide the nail head and joint edges and to stiffen the joint.

Your pattern should cross the nail head at least twice in each direction to form an X and should go around each arm of the joint at least once. The pattern should end on the hoop and then cross behind the leg; then spiral around the hoop until the next joint is reached.

Start the wrapping with a knot or a nail. End the wrap where you wish with a knot or a nail. Then start again if necessary. Make certain your cane is well soaked so that it is soft and pliable. Be careful not to slide the cane through your fingers; the edge of the cane can easily cut you.

When you come to the splices on the hoops, just wrap them closely so as to hide the joint.

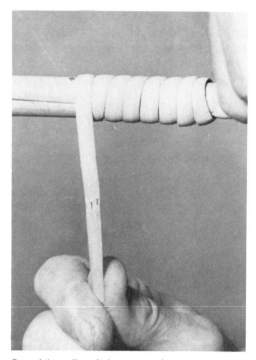

One of the splices being wrapped.

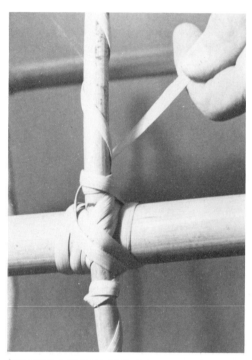

One of the pole-hoop joints being wrapped.

FINAL STEPS
After the cane has thoroughly dried, lock it in place with a few drops of cement placed judiciously here and there.

Position the coffee table frame where you want the table to be. Center the glass on top. Now check for tipping by pushing down on the edge of the glass. If the table tips, try turning the frame. Your floor may be uneven, and since the table legs are not solidly mated to the assembly, the legs can adapt to floor irregularities. If the table still tips, find the short leg. Slip some cardboard under it to determine just how short it is. Then file or sandpaper the high leg or legs by half this amount. If the difference is an eighth of an inch or so, try cementing a thin disk of cork under the short leg.

Indoors, there is nothing more that needs to be done. But if you plan to use the table on a patio or anywhere else where it may occasionally be struck by rain, seal both ends of each leg with a coat of varnish or lacquer or enamel.

10
COFFEE TABLE (DESIGN TWO)

PARTS LIST		
Arms	2 pieces 1¼-inch rattan pole, 50 inches long
Straight braces	2 pieces ¾-inch rattan pole, 30 inches long
Arch Braces	2 pieces ¾-inch rattan pole, 60 inches long
Glass top	$\frac{5}{16}$-inch inch plate, 30 inches in diameter
Binding cane	15 feet
Wood screws	8 1¼-inch #8 flathead
	4 1-inch #8 flathead

The coffee table pictured is 19 inches high. The design can be interpreted as modern, Deco, or native. It will blend well with almost any room. The circular plate glass top is 30 inches across. The glass rests in steps cut into the tops of the main arches, or arms. When necessary, the glass can be lifted up and out and the two parts of the table transported separately.

**DESIGN AND CONSTRUCTION
VARIATIONS**

This design cannot be varied very much without actually going into an entirely different design. But some small changes are practical. As it stands, the bottoms of the main arms are clear of the floor by 1 inch. You could, if you wished, vary this distance, raising the arms or lowering them until they rested on the floor. The arch braces do not touch the bottom of the glass. There is a clearance of about 1 inch. This too could be altered one way or another.

The main arms are made of 1¼-inch rattan. You could go to thicker poles if you wished without any structural change. But if you use 1-inch poles, you should provide cross bracing.

Should you use cross braces, they can be made from ¾-inch rattan. The best way to install them is to crisscross from near the top of one arm to the top of the opposite arm. The braces should be fastened with screws to the arm ends and to each other where they cross. The braces can be positioned in contact with the underside of the glass or just a fraction of an inch below.

The reason cross bracing is required with 1-inch rattan arms is that the arms hold the glass by virtue of their natural spring. The arms press inward against the edges of the glass. While the 1-inch rattan can also maintain sufficient pressure for the job, the thicker poles are more dependable and steadier.

MAKING THE MAIN ARMS

Start by carefully measuring the diameter of the round glass top you plan to use for the coffee table. The measurements given are for a table with a glass top 30 inches in diameter. If the glass you use is larger or smaller, you will, of course, have to alter the following dimensions accordingly. Read through the full instructions first so you understand the relationships of the measurements given.

Draw with chalk on your workboard a rectangle 28 inches long and 18 inches wide. Then draw an arc inside the rectangle with the arc's center touching the center of one long side; the ends of the arc are made tangent with the short sides. The arc is the shape to which you have to bend the poles forming the main arms. Fasten guides to the workboard to outline the arc.

Measure the diameter of the glass disk very carefully. The entire design is pitched to this dimension.

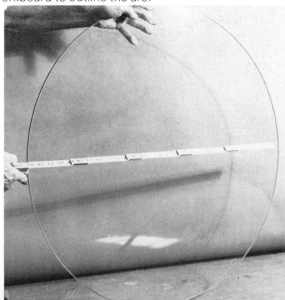

Bending the arms   Each arm pole is 50 inches long before bending. The bend is straightforward, but it will take a little time. The poles are fairly thick and the radius of the arcs are fairly large, which means you have to swing the torch over several feet of pole at one time, which makes for slow heating. But no matter, keep a steady pull on the pole and you will bend it. When doing so, try to keep the last 3 inches of each end of the arc unbent, parallel to the other end, so that it will be at right angles to the floor when the table is completed. In other words, the arc you need is somewhat like the letter *U*. You want 25½ inches between the facing surfaces of the completed arm. This is necessary because you want the arms to press inward against the edges of the glass.

One arm bent, bend a second one as close to identical to the first as you can. Then, using the sketch guide on your workboard, cut both arms to size, making certain before you do that the center of the arc is centered between the arms. If you are uncertain of just how long the arms should be, just cut a little off at a time and see how they work out.

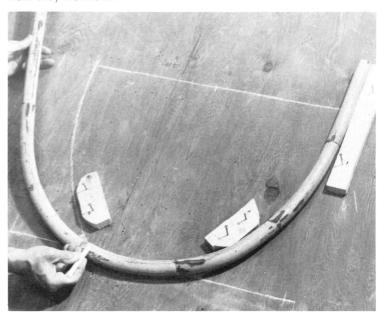

The pieces of wood, or cleats, outline the desired curve. Chalk is being used to mark the spot at which additional heat and pressure need to be applied.

Erecting the arms   With string, chalk, and a nail, make a compass and draw a circle on the workboard. Make the diameter of the circle equal to the diameter of the table's glass top. In our case, this is 30 inches.

Invert the two arches atop the workboard. Fasten a piece of scrap lumber across the tops of the two arches, using clamps or tape to hold the two arms vertical. Position the two arms so that their ends are centered over the chalk line outlining the circle. See that the two arms are perfectly vertical. When they are, check again to see whether or not each leg is centered over the chalk line.

(Remember, the line represents the glass top. This is where the glass will go, and you want the arms to hold it firmly.) If the arm ends are a little within the circle, fine. If they are outside the circle, you have three options: You can tighten each bend to pull the arm ends together. You can shorten the legs a little, in which case you will be closer to the center of the arc and the arm spread will be less. Or you can move the arms toward each other, in which case the arm ends will be brought inside the circle.

As the table now stands the arms are 12½ inches apart, pole center to pole center. And, of course, the arms are parallel with each other.

When you have made these adjustments and the arms are as they should be and where they should be, lock their ends in position by nailing pieces of wood around each leg where it rests on the workboard. Leave in place the temporary brace holding the two arms together.

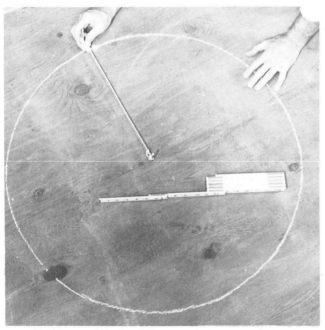

Draw a circle of the same diameter as the glass with the aid of a chalk-string-and-nail compass.

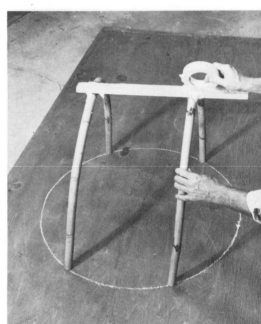

The arms are inverted, their ends positioned over the chalk circle and then held upright with scrap lumber fastened with masking tape.

MAKING AND FASTENING THE STRAIGHT BRACES

The two straight ¾-inch rattan poles are straight braces. They hold the arch braces, which are also legs, in place. Each straight brace is 27 inches long on the completed table, but it is suggested that you start with 30-inch pieces.

Each brace is fastened to the arms exactly 16½ inches above the workboard. Which means that when the table is placed in its proper position, the straight braces will be 4 inches from the floor.

Right now the arms are inverted, so measure upward 16½ inches, center the brace over the two arms. Clamp one end of the brace to an arm and then drill the other end where it abuts the other arm for a 1⅛-inch #8 screw. Then do the same with the other end of the same brace. Fasten the second straight brace in place the same way.

Next, with a pencil, mark the width of each brace on the arm where it contacts the arm. Remove one brace. Chamfer each arm between the pencil marks to a depth of about ¼ inch. Insert the straight brace in the grooves and replace the screws. Repeat with the second brace.

The ends of the arms have been locked in place with pieces of wood. Now one straight brace is clamped in position.

While a screw holds one end of this straight brace in position, its other end is positioned with the aid of a ruler.

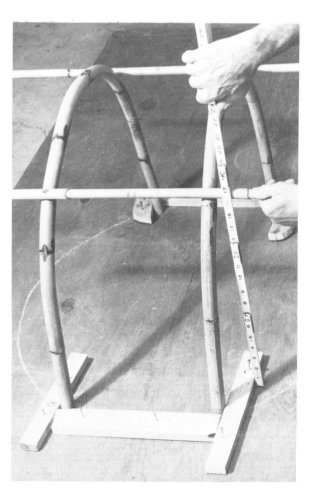

MAKING AND FASTENING THE ARCH BRACES

Each arch brace is made of ¾-inch rattan and starts out 60 inches long. This is a little longer than necessary, but it leaves you room for corrections and change.

Bending

Start by drawing another rectangle on your workboard. Make it 28 inches long and 17½ inches wide. Now draw an arc starting at one corner of the rectangle and reaching around to the facing corner on the far side. Outline the curve you have drawn with some scraps of wood.

Then try the rattan pole and see how far you can bend it cold. Then apply heat as necessary. If possible, let the ends of the rattan project beyond the rectangle. This will give you a longer brace should you need a few more inches. One pole bent, bend a second one. This should be close to the first in shape, but it does not have to be as close in shape as the two arms are to each other.

Place a 1-inch-thick piece of wood on the workboard midway between one pair of ends of the inverted arms. This piece of wood is a spacer. Next, place one arch brace atop the spacer and inside the two arms. The center of the arch brace should be centered between the arms and resting on the spacer. Fasten the arch brace to the arm with 1¼-inch #8 screws — or clamp the arch to the legs with masking tape or carpenter's clamps, and later, when you are certain all is as it should be, fasten the arch brace to the arms.

Repeat this performance at the other ends of the two arms using the second arch brace.

Next, fasten the arch braces to the straight braces. This can be done with a pin joint or a small screw. To make the pin joint drill a ³⁄₁₆-inch hole through both pieces of rattan. Then slide a short piece of reed, covered with a little glue, through the holes. Later cut the reed flush with the rattan. When the joint is wrapped, the reed is doubly fixed in position. If you use screws, use a 1-inch #8 flathead wood screw.

While the table is still in its inverted position, you can check the ends of each arch brace and cut them to the same length. The arch braces, of course, serve as the table's legs when the table is right side up. And that is the next step. If you haven't already done so, remove the temporary piece of wood holding the arms together and turn the table right side up. Now you can remeasure the legs to see that they are truly the same length. Now you can double-check to see that the legs or arch braces are in the same relative position to each other where they are fastened to the straight braces.

WRAPPING THE JOINTS

With the exception of the joints between the straight braces and the arms, all the joints are wrapped. There is nothing special about these wrappings. The cane is brought over the joint crisscross fashion in both directions two or more times. That does it. You will need about 15 feet of cane in all.

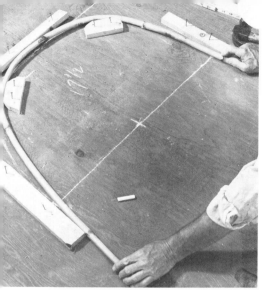

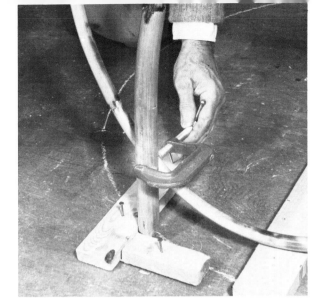

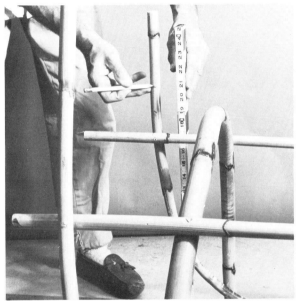

TOP LEFT: Making an arch brace.

TOP RIGHT: Temporarily fastening an arch brace to the arms. The piece of wood beneath the arch serves as a spacer.

ABOVE LEFT: A pilot hole is being drilled through the end of one straight brace preparatory to joining the two braces with a wood screw. Note the position of the two braces in relation to the main arms.

ABOVE RIGHT: The ends of the arch braces—which serve as legs—are now cut to their proper length. This is best done in stages; cut a little, right the table, and try.

RIGHT: The table is now right side up. Leg height is checked with a ruler. Remember, the tops of the arms must also be close to the same height. If you have to make a choice, let the legs vary a little rather than the arm ends.

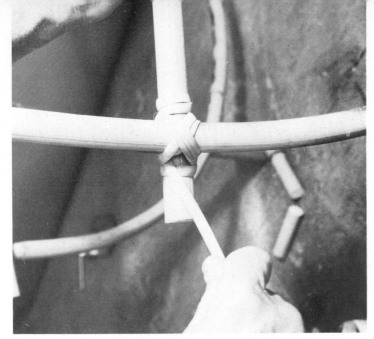

One of the joints is being wrapped.

POSITIONING THE GLASS   With a ruler and pencil carefully mark the desired final height of the table on each leg. Measure up from the floor, in this case the workboard, taking care to keep the ruler as vertical as possible. In this particular case, the finished height of the table is 19 inches, so the marks were made exactly 18¾ inches above the workboard. Next, each arm end is sawed halfway through right on top of the mark. Each time the saw blade is held parallel to the floor, tangent to what will be the circumference of the glass disk (that is to be supported), and inside the facing arm ends. All this sounds complicated, but if you examine the illustrations and think about how the glass will rest between the table's arms, the position of the was cuts will be obvious. You will find it much easier to make these cuts if you place each arm flat against the workboard.

Next, use a kitchen knife and split the ends of the arms down to the saw cuts. Remove the pieces of wood loosened by the knife.

Lower the glass into place on the steps you have cut into the arm ends. If you have to spread the arms to fit the glass, you are ready for the next step. If the arms do not press against the glass, remove the glass. Place the table on its side, arm ends on the floor and then push down hard on the other ends of the arms. Doing so will bring the arm ends together a little. Try the glass again. If the fit is still very loose, find a heavy friend to push down on the arms while you apply wet heat to the bends.

There must be pressure between the arms against the glass. If there isn't, moisture variations can cause the arms to spread sufficiently and possibly permit the glass to fall. If for some reason you cannot get the arms to come together sufficiently by bending them this way, you can either disassemble the table and rebend the arms or you can pull them together with ½- to ¾-inch-thick poles connecting the arms diagonally.

Mark the top of the coffee table on one arm end. The mark has to be carried around to the inside of the arm where the cut will be made.

Cut the step that will hold and support the edge of the glass.

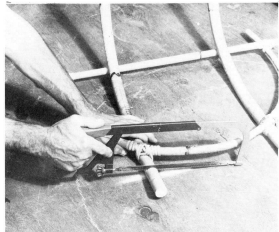

Split the top end of an arm to make the necessary step support for the glass.

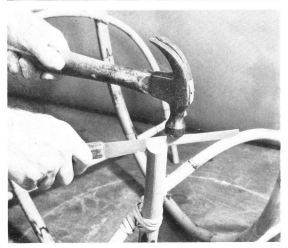

The glass is positioned. The fit should be better than snug. It should be necessary to push the arms apart a little.

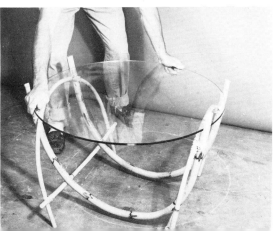

FINISHING UP   With the glass disk properly supported, mark the arm ends where they project above the glass. Cut the arm ends off and then round them a little with a file or Surform plane.

Seal all the cut rattan ends and silicon-free bend areas with clear enamel or varnish, and you are done.

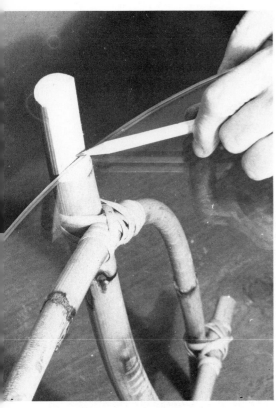

The position of the top surface of the glass is marked on the end of the arm. Then the glass is removed and the arm cut along the pencil mark.

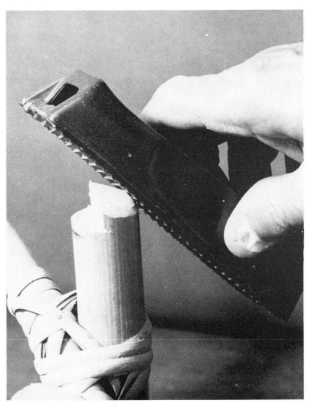

The pole end is rounded. Note the step that holds the glass.

11
CLOTHES TREE

PARTS LIST		
Pole	1 pieces 1 + -inch rattan pole, 56 inches long
Crossbars	2 pieces ¾-inch rattan pole, 24 inches long
Legs	3 pieces ¾-inch rattan pole, 36 inches long
Hooks	2 pieces ½-inch rattan pole, 12 inches long
	2 pieces ½-inch rattan pole, 14 inches long
Wood screws	9 1½-inch #8 flathead
Nails	12 4-penny finishing
Binding cane	100 inches (for a 1½-inch center pole)

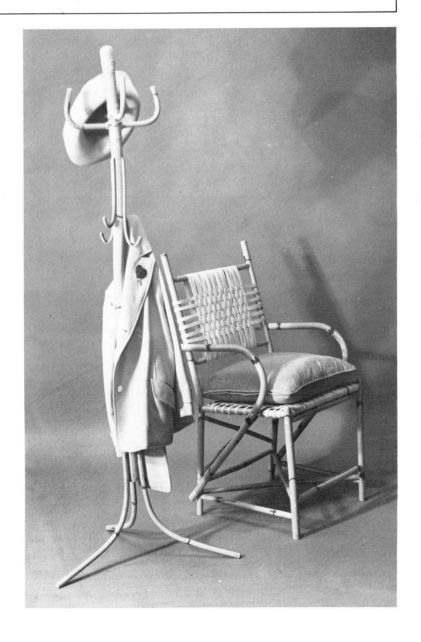

Not only is the clothes tree pictured here unique, but it is a member of a vanishing race. So if you do choose to build one or more clothes trees, you will have furniture few others have.

As it stands, it is 69 inches overall. Its three legs spread a distance of 26 inches and its crossbars spread 12 inches. The center pole is 1½ inches thick and 56 inches long. Three-quarter-inch stock is used for the legs and crossbars. The hooks are made of ½-inch rattan stock. Reed will not do.

You can, if you wish, use a thinner center pole. In that case, you can support the crossbars within deep grooves. Any pole thickness down to 1 inch will do. If you wish, you can use four legs or even more, which would make this tree even more treelike and unusual. But do not make the legs or crossbars of anything less than ¾-inch stock. The tree will be too springy.

Of course you can make the tree shorter or taller; move the position of the crossbars and add or decrease the number of hooks.

Construction is simple and straightforward. Hot bending is necessary, but none of the bends is anything near critical. The crossbars are most difficult, but you do not have to make the tips of their hooks point backward. They can simply be right angles and still look good and do their job.

MAKING THE CENTER POLE

The pole that was used for the illustrated tree was crooked when purchased. No attempt was made to straighten it. To this furniture craftsman, at least, it looked good the way it was, so that was the way it was left. Anyway, it is very difficult to do anything with 1½-inch rattan poles.

Finishing the top end

You can, if you wish, simply clean up the rough edges of the cut and let the pole be. Or, you can round it with a plane and file, or you can wrap it, as shown. (The technique used to wrap the end of the pole is discussed and illustrated in chapter 5.) The lower end of the pole is merely relieved, which means that sandpaper is used to remove the fuzz and rough edges left by the saw.

Two holes are drilled at right angles to each other, one 9 inches the other 10½ inches down from the top of the pole.

Making the holes

You will need 1-inch holes through the pole if you bend the ¾-inch crossbars before you insert them. It is possible to bend the bars after they have been passed through the holes in the pole. If this is done, you can probably get by with a smaller hole. But the extra effort is not worth the results. There will still be a large opening between the crossbars and the holes and you will still need to wrap the joints to hide the openings.

In any case, make the highest hole about 9 inches down from the top of the pole and make the second hole at right angles to the first and 1½ inches farther down. (Both holes must be parallel to the floor when the pole is upright.)

MAKING THE CROSSBARS

Each crossbar is made from a pole at least 24 inches long. A little longer pole will cost you material but will make the bending a little easier, especially if this is one of your first projects.

Making a pattern and a jig, or guide

On your workboard draw a rectangle in chalk 12 inches by 5 inches. Within the sides of the rectangle, draw two facing curves.

Make a guide by fastening three pieces of lumber ⅜ inch from the outside of three sides of the rectangle.

Draw the pattern for the crossbars. The rectangle is 12 by 5 inches. Then nail guide boards around three sides of the pattern, clear of the drawing by half the thickness of the pole that is to be fitted inside.

Bending the bars

Use ¾-inch scant stock. ("Scant" means it can be a fraction less.) Place 2 or so inches of the pole end inside your vise. Apply water and heat. Confine the heat to a small area so as to make a tight (small-radius) bend. Bring the end of the pole down and as close to the vise as you can; this will bring the end of the pole back toward itself a bit. If not, it doesn't matter, the bar end can point straight up just as well.

This done, try the bent piece of rattan in your jig. See how it fits. Then mark the center of the bend you require at the other end of the crossbar. This time, place the other end of the same pole in the vise, taking care to position the center-of-the-desired-bend mark where you want it. Heat and bend.

If you find the two ends of the bar are not parallel, place one end in the vise and pull the other into alignment. Use a little heat if necessary.

Now try the completed crossbar in the guide. If it is a little smaller, or if one end projects beyond the guide, no matter. Cut what is necessary and simply make the second bar the same size as the first bar.

When the bars are completed, round off their ends. If you have a power grindstone, use it; it will save a lot of filing and sanding.

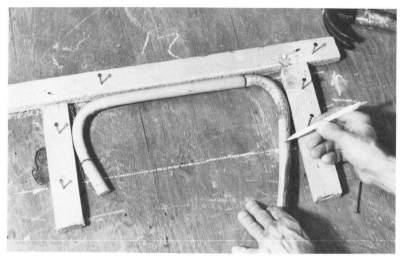

One crossbar has been bent out of a longer than needed piece of rattan. The necessary cuts are marked with a pencil.

MAKING THE LEGS   Each leg is made of ¾-inch rattan, preferably full (meaning the full ¾ inch or a bit more). One-inch-thick legs will make the tree even stiffer, but they are much more difficult to bend. Each leg is about 36 inches long. There is no need for any additional "safety" length here. The bend is a simple right angle. If the upper end of the leg comes out a bit short, it is merely fastened lower down on the pole.

With chalk, draw a rectangle on your workboard 32 inches long and 12¼ inches wide. (We use chalk because it is easily removed with a wet cloth.) Freehand a curve at one end. Next, outline the curve with blocks of wood leaving a space of little more than ¾ inch between them. This is for gauging the leg curves.

If they fit the space, the curve is correct. If not, it's back to the vise and blowtorch.

Bending   Nineteen inches of the leg must be straight, or reasonably straight. So, measure this distance in from either end of the leg. Mark this point with a pencil. Open your vise and position the leg vertically between its jaw so that the 19-inch mark is flush with the

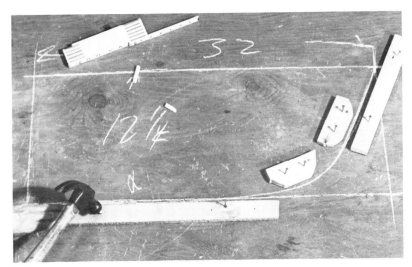

Draw the pattern for the legs. This rectangle is 32 inches by 12¼ inches. The curve can be done freehand. Then nail guide boards around the pattern. Note that only a few boards are needed. Two short, somewhat rounded pieces of wood limit the inside of the curve; two straight, longer boards limit the outside of the curve. Note the space left between the guide boards—actually the setup is a gauge—for the rattan pole.

top of the jaws and the portion of the leg that is not to be bent is below the top edge of the vise jaws. Now close the jaws of the vise on the leg. This is the way you keep as much of a leg from bending as you wish.

The last portion of the leg, the portion that will rest on the floor, should be straight too, so slip about 3 inches of the upper end of the vertical leg inside a length of pipe. Now when you heat and bend the leg, 19 inches of one end will remain straight while about 3 inches of the other end will also be unaffected by the bending.

Since you want a fairly large-radius bend or curve in the leg, swing your torch flame over the area between the vise and pipe end while you apply pressure. Hold the pressure and watch the curve. Where the rattan is loath to give, apply a little more heat. On a right-angle bend of this sort you can generally quit when the leg has been bent almost back on itself. In any case, when you have permitted the leg to cool and the bend looks right, try the bent leg in your jig. If it is close, make the final correction cold. Just put it under your foot and push or pull as necessary.

Now you can go on to making the rest of the legs.

Finishing   Taper the top end of each leg so that the end will not protrude when it is fastened to the center pole. Then drill and countersink three holes in the long, straight portion of each leg. Use a drill and countersink suitable for 1½-inch #8 screws. Relieve all the leg edges with sandpaper or a file.

MAKING THE HOOKS   The hooks are made by hot-bending ½-inch rattan and then cutting a portion of the bend off so that a semicircle results. Two hooks are made from 12-inch-long pieces of rattan, and two are made from 14-inch stock. If you examine the photo, you will see that the upper ends of the four hooks are at the same level, but that their lower ends are at two different levels. This is because it is usually easier to hang coats and whatnot if the hooks are not all side by side.

ASSEMBLY

Installing the crossbars

Start by slipping one of the crossbars through a hole in the pole. Add glue to the inside of the hole. Center the crossbar in the hole. See that the two ends point straight up. Fill the space between the bar and the inside of the hole with wedges of wood. Use the wedges to correct for whatever inaccuracies may exist in the hole. Make the wedges tight, but not so tight you split the pole. Then do the same with the second crossbar.

Give the glue a good day or more to harden, then, with a hacksaw, carefully cut the wedges flush to the surface of the pole. If there are any large openings remaining, fill them, if you wish, with putty darkened a little with artist's oil color. Ocher probably produces the best match.

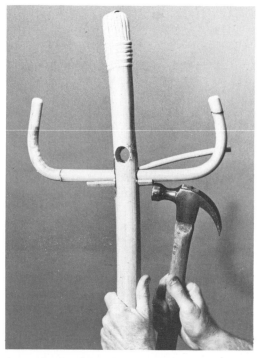

A crossbar has been slipped through one hole in the center pole. Now glue and wedges are added.

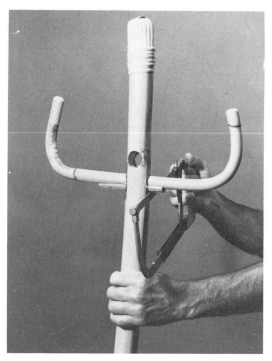

The wedges are cut flush with the side of the pole. (This was done one crossbar at a time for photographic clarity.)

Wrapping the joints

Start the binding cane an inch or more below the lowest crossbar. Circle the pole until you come to the crossbar, then crisscross around it so as to hide the joint and wedge ends. Then circle the pole, crisscross over the next crossbar, and finish with a few turns around the pole.

The crossbars are wrapped.

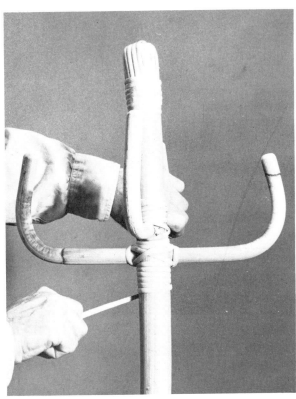

Fastening the legs   Divide the circumference of the pole into three or more sections: one for each leg. Mark the divisions with a pencil. Place one leg atop a pencil mark so that the leg is in line with the pole and the top of the leg is 18 inches or so up from the bottom of the pole. Drill a pilot hole through the predrilled holes in the leg. Use a $\frac{9}{64}$-inch bit and make a hole in the center pole $\frac{3}{4}$ inch or so deep. Then fasten the leg to the pole with $1\frac{1}{2}$-inch #8 screws. Repeat with the other legs.

The legs are fastened to the center pole. You need a pilot hole in the rattan. Without it you will have great difficulty in starting the screws.

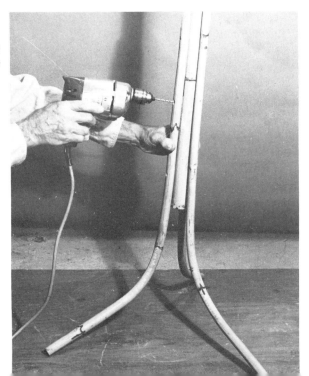

Fastening the hooks

The hooks are nailed in place with their top ends in line with one another and 14 inches below the top of the pole. Each hook is vertical, equidistant from its neighbor, and positioned below the space between the crossbars. Three 4-penny finishing nails are all that are needed for each hook. Don't drive the nails flush with the surface of the rattan, since you may split the wood.

FINAL ADJUSTMENTS AND TOUCHES

Leveling

Place the tree on a level floor. If it does not stand reasonably upright, see which leg is at fault. If the bend is too open or too closed, *remove the leg* and then bend it in the desired direction. Do not attempt to correct the bend while the leg is attached to the pole. You may very well rip it loose.

If all that is necessary is that a leg be shortened a fraction, try filing a little from its bottom edge.

Finishing

Go over all the cut pole ends and bends with sandpaper. Seal the cut ends and where the silicon has fallen from the rattan with enamel or any other suitable clear finish.

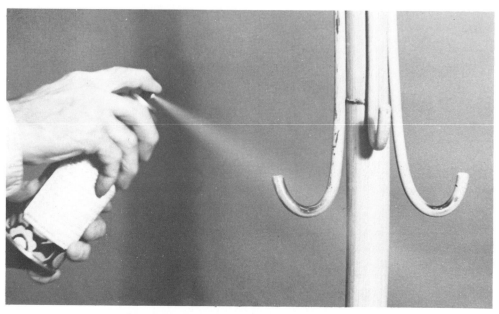

The hooks have been nailed to the center pole. Tops of the hooks are about 14 inches below the top of the pole. Now the ends on the hooks, all the other bends where the silicon has been broken off, and all the raw ends are sealed with a clear enamel or a similar finish.

12
BED BENCH

PARTS LIST		
Seat	1 piece ¾-inch chipboard, 14 by 30 inches	
	1 piece tight cane webbing, 14 by 32 inches	
	2 pieces 1-inch rattan pole, 31½ inches long	
	2 pieces 1-inch rattan pole, 15 inches long	
	1 piece ⅜-inch rattan pole or reed,	
	95 inches long	
Legs	4 pieces 1-inch rattan pole, 30 inches long	
Braces	¾-inch rattan pole	
	2 pieces, 29 inches long	
	2 pieces, 50 inches long	
Wood screws	24 1¼-inch #8 flathead	
	24 1½-inch #8 flathead	
Nails	10 6-penny finishing	
	20 1-inch #16	
Binding cane	20 feet wide	
Handles	2 pieces 1-inch rattan pole, 16½ inches long	

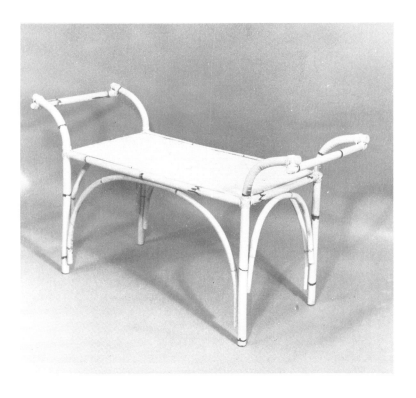

Bed benches are used in bedrooms, where they are positioned at the foot of the bed to provide resting places for night blankets and people who don't like to sit on their beds when putting their shoes on. But with slight modifications the same basic design can be adapted for a utility bench, foot rest, dressing-table chair, utility stool, and even a coffee table.

As it now stands, the top of the seat is 18 inches above the floor. The seat itself is 32 by 16 inches and the overall length of the bench is 44 inches.

DESIGN VARIATIONS

Utility bench

Seat height and other dimensions can remain the same. The curved legs that rise above the seat to support the handles are replaced by legs that do not protrude above the top of the seat. The present handles that also act as leg braces are replaced by horizontal braces that tie the bottoms of the legs together. In addition, cross braces and front and rear braces should be installed.

Thus as a utility bench you would have four straight legs terminating flush with the top of the seat; four braces outlining a rectangle that would go from leg to leg, positioned about 2 inches above the floor; (the lower the braces the more effective they are) and two diagonal braces connecting the four legs and fastened to each other with a wood screw where they crossed. Three-quarter-inch rattan and 1½-inch #8 screws should be used.

Foot rest

The curved legs would be replaced by straight legs some 14 inches long—shorter if you planned to place a cushion atop the foot rest. Seat size would be reduced to perhaps 16 by 16 inches. Since the legs are to be shortened and no one, presumably, is going to drop themselves down onto the foot rest as people often do when sitting down on a chair, there is no need for braces in addition to those used with the bed bench.

Dressing-table seat

The curved legs might be left in place or replaced by straight legs. The seat could be reduced to 16 by 20 inches or so—it is all a matter of taste. Seat height could remain the same or be increased a few inches to bring the little lady in better view of her mirror.

If the curved legs and handles are retained in the design and the legs are not lengthened, no more bracing is needed. If the handles are removed and the legs increased, four horizontal bars forming a square or rectangle should be added.

Coffee table

After you have shortened the legs to bring the top of the seat down to the usual coffee table height of 17 inches, the only additional design change would depend on whether you want to cover the cane webbing with varnish or glass.

If you elected to go with glass, you would be well advised to purchase the glass plate first and then build the table around it. The only structural change in the design would be the elimination of the ⅜-inch rattan edging. If you build first and then have the glass cut to size, the cost of the glass may very well be considerably higher.

If you opt for varnish, apply a great many coats, allowing each coat plenty of time to dry hard. If you simply pour it on, the varnish or whatever may never dry. Incidentally, use a brush rather than a spray can. For this purpose the spray can is much too expensive.

Bear in mind that you have to fill all the cracks and crevices with the varnish or clear enamel. Otherwise, crumbs and soil will soon darken the table top, no matter how hard you may work at cleaning it afterward.

MAKING THE SEAT

Begin with a piece of chipboard, ¾ inch thick, 14 inches wide, and 30 inches long. Although chipboard is not as strong as plywood or pine, it is best for this purpose. Plywood will not take edge screws very well. Clean pine 14 inches wide is astronomical in cost, and #2 pine, which means it has tight knots, is also very expensive. Both are difficult to get, since few lumberyards carry them. If you do choose to use the pine, be certain to shellac the knots and then varnish all sides and edges of the board. If you do not do this, there is a good chance the board will warp and crack.

In any case, have the yard cut the chipboard or pine for you. Unless you are an experienced carpenter, this is the only way you can be certain of square corners and edges.

Applying the webbing

Purchase a piece of tightly woven cane webbing 14 inches wide and 32 inches long. Soak it for several hours in lukewarm water. Apply a thin layer of Elmer's glue to one side of the chipboard. Use a table knife to make certain there is glue on the entire board. Use special care to make certain there is glue at the corners

Use a bread knife to spread glue over one side of the seat board.

Press the well-soaked cane webbing smoothly onto the glue-covered seat board. Cover with brown paper and weights and let dry.

and edges of the board. Place the cane webbing on top of the board, shiny side of the webbing up. With your hand or a board flatten the webbing and press it tightly down against the clipboard. Rip a number of brown paper bags open and spread them over the webbing. (Do not use newspaper, since the ink may come off.) Place boards and weights on top of the paper to hold the webbing flat and in place. Give it all at least a full day to dry hard.

Cutting the webbing

Place the seat board, webbing side down, on top of your workboard. With a razor knife trim the webbing flush with the sides of the board. Take care not to pull any cane free of the board.

Trimming the corners

This design calls for wrapped corners where the legs join the seat. To facilitate wrapping and to take care of the legs themselves, the corners are cut back at an angle. Measure inward at a diagonal from each corner about ¾ inch and cut the seat vertically at that point with a hacksaw.

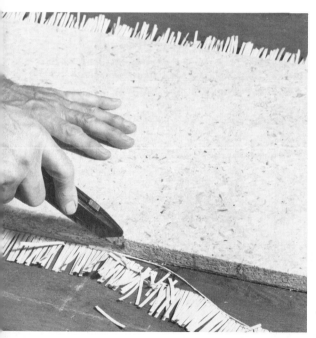

When the cane webbing has dried and the glue has set, turn the board over and trim the excess webbing. Note that the 14-inch-wide webbing is actually several inches wider but not woven to its edge.

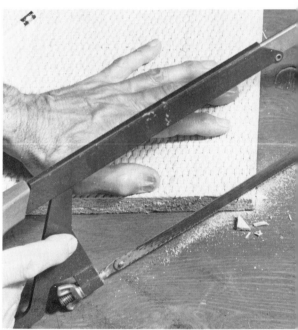

Trim the corners of the seat board with a hacksaw.

Making the seat's sides

The long sides of the seat are "framed" by 1-inch poles. Each pole is carefully cut to a length of 31½ inches. The end of each pole is then cut down to a diameter of ⅝ inch for a distance of ¾ inch. This can be done with a knife and a file or even with the aid of a grindstone. (The dark ring around one pole end in the illustration was left by a grindstone.) But no matter how you reduce the end diameter of the pole, remove less wood than necessary at this time. Later you will cut the pole ends down to final diameter. As you can see, we are going to make four mortise-and-tenon joints. These will take the vertical load — the weight on the seat.

Next, use the Surform plane or a coarse file and remove the lumps and bumps along one side of each pole. We want these poles to fit snugly alongside the seat board.

This done, drill three or four ⅛-inch holes through each pole. Place the seat board, webbing up, on your workboard. Place the poles alongside the seat board. Align them so that there is just as much pole projecting beyond one end of the board as the other. Drive 6-penny finishing nails through the holes in the poles and into the sides of the board.

You now have a board covered with a layer of webbing, its four corners cut off and attached by nails to two poles. Note that the top edges of the poles project above the top surface of the webbing. So far so good.

Next drill and countersink pilot holes through the poles and into the board. Drill for 1½-inch #8 screws. Drive the screws home. Three screws a pole are plenty. Countersink (drive below the surface) the nails. They were used to hold the poles in place for drilling and screwing.

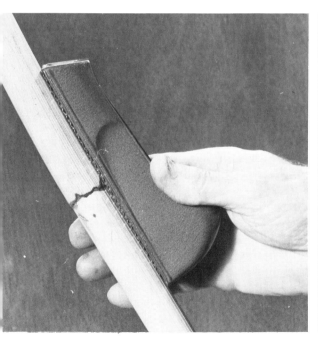
Remove the lumps and bumps from the sides of the poles that will contact the side of the seat board. This is to make a closer fit possible.

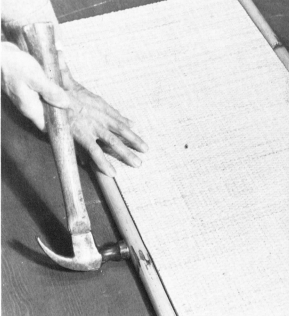
Small-diameter holes are drilled through the poles that are to be fastened to the seat board. Finishing nails are then used to align the side poles with the seat board. Note that the tenons start flush with the end of the seat board.

MAKING THE LEGS

The legs are made from 30-inch pieces of 1-inch rattan. But it is advisable to start with poles a couple of inches longer. They will be easier to bend.

Start by drawing a rectangle on your workboard 8½ by 20 inches in size. The pattern for the leg will fit into this rectangle. Frame the rectangle with scrap lumber on three sides, leaving a short side open. Place the wood adjacent to the chalk lines. Draw a curve within one end of the rectangle. Make this curve something less than a right angle.

Bending

Place the pole vertically in the vise with 4 inches of pole below the top edge of the vise jaws. Wet, heat, and bend, taking care to keep the heat and bend near the vise. You want a small-radius curve. When you believe you have the desired curve, try the rattan in your guide. If the end of the pole projects beyond the guide, that is good. If it is short of the guide, that is bad. You have either to discard the pole or bend again. The reason for this is that you may have inserted too much of the pole in the vise. The result is extra pole at the curved end.

In any event, when you have bent one pole satisfactorily, cut it to size; fit it into the guide and then fasten a small curved block of wood to the workboard, inside the curve of the pole. Fasten a second, straight board alongside the straight portion of the leg. Remove the leg. Now you have a gauge you can use to help you bend the remaining three poles to the same curve and size.

Drilling the holes in the legs

Form a right angle with two pieces of scrap lumber on your workboard. Make certain the angle is as nearly perfect as possible by adjusting the boards with a try square or combination square. Nail the boards lightly to the workboard.

Place one bent-and-cut-to-size bench leg on your workboard. Place its side against one piece of scrap lumber, its end against the other piece of lumber. Place the second leg alongside the first; its handle pointing away from the first leg, the bottom touching the same board that the bottom of the first touches. The second leg should be as parallel to the first as possible. Do the same with the remaining two legs. Now, let us call the board touching the ends of the legs the floor. With your try square make each leg as vertical to the "floor" as you can. Remember, you must allow for bends and curves in the legs. That is always the problem when working with rattan.

Next, measure up from the "floor" board exactly 17½ inches. Mark this point on the other piece of scrap lumber. Next, carry this mark across all four legs, taking care to hold the line you draw parallel to the "floor" board.

Now here comes the tricky part. Take each leg in hand in turn and carry the height mark you just made around to the side of the leg *away* from the handle end. Next, place each leg in the vise and drill a ⅞-inch hole in each leg, in line with the height mark, in line with the handle and parallel to what will be the floor when the bench is completed. Make each hole ¾ inch deep. If you think of how the bench will be assembled or examine the side view of the bench you will see exactly how these holes must be drilled. Just take care *not to drill beneath* the handle or curve. That is the wrong side of the leg.

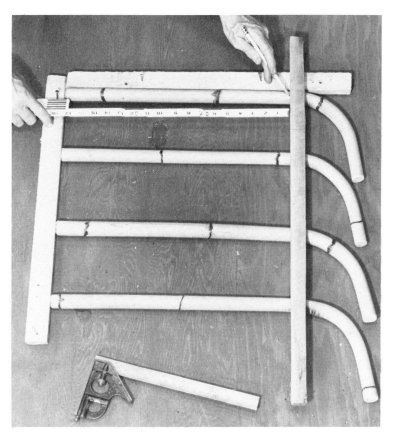

To make certain that each leg is the same length from the seat board down, the legs are aligned as shown and all the mortise hole locations are marked at one time.

PARTIAL ASSEMBLY

Fastening the legs to the seat

. Start by making a right-angle support. Nail a piece of scrap lumber to a second but thicker piece of lumber that has "finished" sides. This simply means that it hasn't been all cut up but its sides are still square and relatively smooth.

Nail the right-angle support to your workboard. (You can see how on page 112.) Place the top side of the seat against the right-angle support. Position one leg so that the mortise (hole) is in line with the tenon of the pole fastened to the seat board. Tap the leg into place. From the side opposite the tenon, drill and countersink a hole through the leg and into the tenon. Remove the leg. Put a little glue in the mortise. Reposition the leg. Fasten it with a 1¼-inch #8 screw.

The purpose of this arrangement, which you will see when you go through the steps, is to keep the leg vertical to the surface of the seat.

Turn the seat around and do the same with a second leg. Since the weight of the upper leg will tilt the seat board, use a clamp to hold it to the right-angle support.

Fasten the remaining two legs in place the same way.

The seat board is held in a vertical position. The leg is forced over the tenon. Then a pilot hole is drilled through the leg into the tenon. A wood screw is then inserted.

A second leg is fastened the same way. Note the right angle support holding the seat board vertical.

Making the ends of the seat

The rattan fastened to the ends of the seat board is cut from 1-inch stock. Each piece is cut ½ inch longer than the space between the legs. Then the ends of the short poles are chamfered and the poles slide between the legs. On this bench you will need two pieces of 1-inch rattan 15 inches long, allowing a fraction of an inch for final cutting.

As before, remove the lumps and bumps on the side of the poles that will contact the side of the seat board. After you have chamfered them to fit between the legs, fasten the poles to the seat board. Three 1¼-inch #8 screws are plenty for each piece.

MAKING AND INSTALLING THE BRACES

At this point you have fastened the four legs to the seat board. The legs are in reasonable alignment with each other and orthagonal—at right angles—to the seat board. Now we have to install the braces that will lock the legs in position. The bed bench pictured utilizes four arch-shape braces. They are not difficult to bend, but they are moderately difficult to hold accurately to size. Since they hold the legs in position, you cannot install oversize or undersize arch braces here, since they will either pull the legs together or push them apart, neither of which is desirable.

The alternative to an arch brace is a pair of right-angle braces. They are not quite as strong but are made a lot more quickly and easily. In any case, the arch braces are discussed first, along with their installation. Then right-angle braces are covered.

The long arch braces   These braces are screwed to the underside of the long sides of the bench.

Begin by drawing three sides of a rectangle exactly 31 by 14 inches on your workboard — leave a long side open. On this bench the 31 inches is the exact distance between the legs on the long side of the bench. The 14 inches is the distance down from the underside of the bench to which the brace ends will go. The second dimension is not at all critical as long as it doesn't exceed the length of the legs. You can vary it by several inches if you wish. But the long dimension is. Vary it and your arch brace will not fit properly.

Draw two large-radius arcs at facing ends of the rectangle. If you are going to use the string and nail bit to make perfect arcs, you will want to make the nail-to-chalk distance — the radius of the arc — about 26 inches.

Outline the three sides of the rectangle with straight pieces of wood. Place the edges of the boards right against the chalk line. Demark the inside of the desired arch brace with two pieces of roughly curved boards fastened to the workboard about 1¼ inches from the inner side of the chalk pattern, more or less in the center of each arc.

You will need a piece of ¾-inch rattan pole 50 or more inches long for each long arch.

The center of the pole should be straight. So center a 6-inch-long space on the pole and mark it with a pencil. The ends of the pole should not be bent either. So measure 3 inches in from each pole end and mark the spot with a pencil.

Position the pole vertically in the vise, with the 3-inch mark flush with the top of the vise. Measure upward to the next mark. Divide this distance in half and make still another mark. This last mark is the more or less exact center of the desired bend.

Wet and heat keeping your eye on the center-of-the-bend mark. Move your torch as necessary and keep bending until you have secured the desired bend. Then put the other end of the pole in the vise, again with the 3-inch mark flush with the top of the vise. Mark the desired center of the bend on this portion of the pole and repeat your heating and bending performance.

This done, try your arch brace in your jig. Bear in mind you want a flat section touching the underside of the seat frame, and a flat section touching each leg. Bend and correct as necessary and, of course, if necessary. Bear in mind that you want the arch brace to just make it. If anything more than a light pull is necessary, the brace will pull the legs out of whack.

Now make the second long arch brace.

This done, place the bench on its side atop your workboard. With a try square, check to make certain each of the two legs lying against the workboard are perfectly square with the underside of the seat board. Adjust as may be necessary. Then fasten a small, straight board to the workboard along the outer sides of each leg. Now the legs are more or less locked in place.

Following this, slip one brace between the legs and into position against the underside of the seat frame. If the brace fits properly, mark it for two screws on top and two screws in each leg. Drill and countersink for 1¼-inch #8 screws.

Holes drilled, the brace is fastened in position. Note that you cannot drive the screw directly into the rattan — you must drill a pilot hole. Use a ⁹⁄₆₄-inch twist drill. Then countersink the hole so that the screwhead is below the surface.

Repeat this operation with the brace on the other side of the bench.

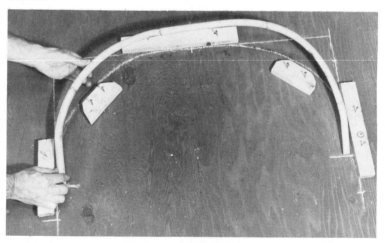

ABOVE: The pattern for the long arch braces is drawn within a rectangle 31 by 14 inches. The wood guides are installed in order to hold the bent rattan pole within this space. Then the bent rattan is tried against the guide.

RIGHT: The seat is on its side. The try square is used to make certain this leg is perfectly square with the seat board. The strip of wood being nailed along the side of the leg will keep the leg from moving out of parallel with the other leg. The same thing is, of course, done with the other leg resting on the workboard.

The short arch braces

With the bench still on its side and both long arches in place, check to make certain the upper legs are parallel to the lower legs. Do this with a ruler or a try square. Now take a length of wood and place it against the bottoms of either pair of legs at the ends of the bench, and drive nails through the wood and partway into the ends of the legs. This will hold the legs a fixed distance apart.

Now, with the two legs fixed, you have a guide that will enable you to bend the small arch braces accurately.

Each arch is made from ¾-inch rattan 29 inches long. As before, mark off the ends that are not to be bent and locate the center of the desired semicircular arc. Then bend and check, bend and check. If the small arch braces are not nearly perfect in size, they too can push the legs out of kilter; so take care.

Each small arch takes five 1¼-inch #8 screws, for which pilot holes are first drilled and countersunk. One at top center, and two in each leg end. Like the long arch, the top of the small arch is screwed to the rattan above it. However, it will abut the rattan above it only at the apex of its curve.

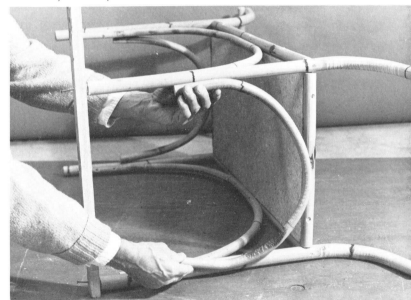

The two legs have been joined by a temporary brace—a piece of wood holding them in perfect alignment, parallel to the workboard. The small arch brace is being tried for size within the space between the legs. The fit must be nearly perfect, or the brace will move the legs out of alignment.

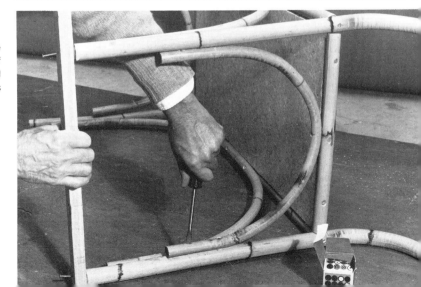

The small brace is fastened to the bench legs and the short side of the seat board pole with wood screws. The board joining the legs is still in place.

Using right-angle braces

Very simply, in place of one arch brace, install two right-angle braces also made of ¾-inch pole stock. Use two wood screws at each end of the brace.

What you might do is start with the arch braces and if you find that they do not come out correctly, cut them in half, shorten one or both if need be, and then install.

FINISHING UP
Attaching the handles

The handles are also made of 1-inch stock. Each handle extends about ¾ inch beyond the leg ends and the leg ends extend an equal distance beyond the handles.

On this bench each handle is 16½ inches long. It is chamfered deeply where it fits beneath the leg. Now, if your leg ends are pointing a bit inward or outward, you can correct this when you install the handles. Use 1¼-inch screws to fasten the handles in place. Round the edges of the handles as well as the edges of the legs once you have fastened them.

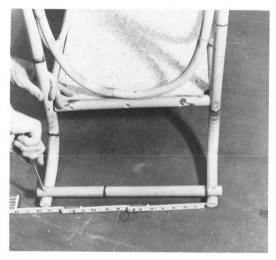

The bench handle is fastened to the underside of the leg tops. The ruler is used to make certain the leg tops are in alignment. Here you can perhaps see more clearly just how the small arch brace is fastened to the pole at the short side of the bench.

Wrapping

The handles are wrapped with a simple crisscross pattern. The wrappings are simply ornamental, nothing more.

The corners, where the legs join the seat are also wrapped for ornamental reasons. Here, the cane is taken around the poles at the sides of the bench board as well as around the leg. This is done to hide the joints. The wrapping passes through the opening that was cut at the corner of the seat at the start of the project.

Installing the trim

The best material to use here is ⅜-inch rattan. If that is not available, use reed of the same diameter, but be certain to varnish it before you nail it in place.

Simply cut lengths to fit the space between the legs and nail the rattan or reed into the groove between the end of the cane webbing and the side of the 1-inch rattan bench sides with 1-inch #16 wire brads. If you are having trouble with the edges of the cane picking up, put down some Duco cement or glue before you position the trim.

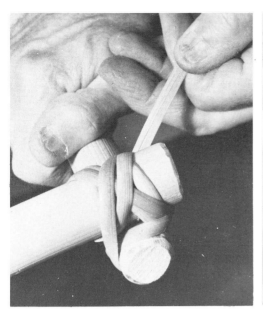

A handle-to-leg joint is being wrapped.

A corner joint is being wrapped. Note how the screw head has been covered with a little colored putty.

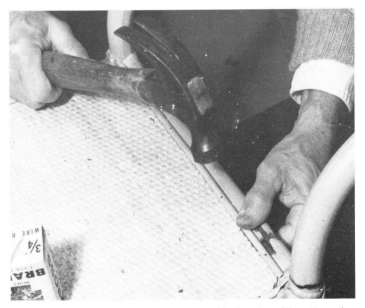

Nail the trim in the groove between the top of the bench and the rattan poles bordering the seat board.

Sealing the ends of the rattan

Clean up the rattan and go over all the cut ends and the bends where the silicon has fallen off with some sort of clear finish.

Sealing the cane webbing

It is a wise move at this time to flood the cane webbing with clear finish of some kind so that all the cracks and crevices are filled. Doing so will keep the soil out and the bench top looking fine and bright for many years to come.

13
ÉTAGÈRE

PARTS LIST		
	Legs	4 pieces 1 + -inch rattan pole, 72 inches long
		2 pieces 1 + -inch rattan pole, 57 inches long
	Shelves	4 pieces ¾-inch chipboard, 29½ by 14 inches
		4 pieces ¾-inch chipboard, 18 by 14 inches
		3½ yards 40-inch-wide burlap
		½ gallon shellac
		½ gallon clear varnish or enamel
	Trim	8 pieces ¾-inch rattan pole, 29 inches long, split in half
		8 pieces ¾-inch rattan pole, 17½ inches long, split in half
		16 pieces ¾-inch rattan pole, 15 inches long, split in half
	Angle braces	13 pieces ¾-inch rattan pole, 18 inches long
	Arch braces	2 pieces ¾-inch rattan pole, 42 inches long
		2 pieces ¾-inch rattan pole, 38 inches long
		1 piece ¾-inch rattan pole, 30 inches long
	Ornamentation	3 pieces 1-inch rattan pole, 15½ inches long
	Ornamental arch braces	2 pieces ¾-inch rattan pole, 35 inches long
	Wood screws	1 box 1½-inch #8 flathead
		1 box 1¼-inch #8 flathead
	Nails	1 package 1¼-inch #16 wire brads

The word is French, and according to Webster, denotes an elaborate whatnot, often with a large mirror at the back and sometimes with an enclosed cabinet at its base. The étagère described herewith has neither the mirror nor the cabinet, but it certainly meets the whatnot requirement.

DESIGN   As it stands, it is 6 feet 1 inch high, 4 feet wide, and 15½ inches deep. The small shelves are 19 inches long. The long shelves are 31 inches long.

Each shelf can carry up to 50 pounds. But the étagère cannot be used as a ladder. The shelves cannot carry a person's weight.

Materials   The vertical poles are 1+ inches thick. The braces are made of ¾-inch poles. The vertical poles can be made up of short sections if they are joined by means of a step splice. Since the load on these poles is almost vertical, step splices are plenty strong.

The shelves are made of ¾-inch chipboard covered with burlap. Cane webbing can be used in place of the burlap, but the cost will be considerably higher.

As here constructed, the étagère is steady and entirely dependable, but it will give a little during an earthquake and if you push it sideways. Should you want your étagère to be rock steady, you will have to add lots more bracing. This is discussed further along. (Additional bracing can always be added.)

Side view of a step splice. This type of joint can carry a heavy vertical load.

Alternate designs   You can make the shelves deeper without problem, but if you make them shallower, you must count on tying the étagère to the wall somehow. One method you might consider consists of a couple of hooks.

You can reduce or increase the height of the unit if you wish. But bear in mind that most ceilings are no more than 8 feet high. Some attic ceilings are only 7 feet high.

Shelves can be made shorter without any design changes. But no shelf should be more than 36 or so inches long between supports. So if you want a 4-foot-long shelf, you would require a middle post as well as posts at the end of the shelf.

Shelf height can be anything you wish. The shelf separation in the unit pictured is 12 and 18 inches respectively as measured from the top of one shelf to the top of the next above. Naturally, the number of shelves installed in your étagère is a matter of taste. But if shelf separation is much less than shelf depth, the shelf looks cramped.

The unit described has a "break" off center with two tiers of short and long shelves at different elevations. The purpose of the two-tier design is both visual and practical. The two tiers look better than would a single tier of longer shelves. Also, with two different shelf lengths and two different shelf heights, you can better display collectibles of different sizes and shapes.

The same system of shelf support and bracing can be used with any arrangement of shelves. The total number of shelves is unimportant. The poles can withstand a tremendous vertical load. It is the shelves themselves that may break in two if much more than 50 pounds or so is placed on any one of them. Chipboard cannot withstand a heavy load that causes it to bend in the middle.

MAKING THE SHELVES

The shelves are made from ¾-inch chipboard, which comes in 4-by-8-foot sheets. Each shelf is 14 inches wide. Four shelves are 18 inches long and four are 29½ inches long. Chipboard can be cut with an ordinary wood saw, but you are well advised to have the lumberyard cut the shelf boards for you. They have a bench saw and can cut the boards far more accurately than anyone can. It is important that the shelves be cut square with smooth straight edges.

Applying the burlap

Each piece of burlap is approximately 2 to 3 inches longer and wider than each shelf board. In all, some 3½ yards of 40-inch-wide material will be needed. You will also need about ½ gallon of shellac with which to glue the burlap in place and seal its openings.

Orange shellac was used on the shelves shown, but the shellac was old, which is the reason the burlap is so dark. If you want a lighter color use fresh white shellac.

Start by cutting the burlap to size. Then press each piece of material with a hot steam iron. You want the burlap as smooth as possible.

Cover your workshop floor with newspapers. Place the shelves on the paper. Place the burlap on each board. Pour a little shellac on each piece of burlap, one at a time. Spread the shellac with a small flat stick. Give the burlap all the shellac it will soak up, and push the shellac about 1 inch past all the edges. Give the shellac enough time to dry hard. Meanwhile, open the windows. Fumes from drying shellac can knock a man or woman down.

The steam-pressed burlap is placed on top of the shelf board and is glued in place by pouring shellac over the cloth and spreading the shellac with a small board.

CUTTING THE POLES You need four 1+-inch poles 72 inches long and two poles of the same thickness 57 inches long. In this design all the poles project above the top shelf by some 7 inches. If you do not want this, you can use shorter poles.

In any case, do not use poles less than 1 inch thick and select poles as straight as possible. Then spend some time taking out whatever bends there may be in the poles, or as much of the bends as you can.

Fasten a long straight-edge board to your workboard. Then fasten a small straight-edge board to your workboard near one end of the long board and at right angles to it. Lay all six legs on your workboard alongside the long board and butted up against the short board, which we call the floor board.

Each shelf is carried in a slot cut into the poles, or étagère legs. In order to hold each shelf perfectly horizontal, each slot must be the proper distance from the floor end of the poles.

So, we place the two short legs alongside the long board, and then the four long legs alongside them. Then we make certain all six legs touch the floor board and all six legs or poles are as parallel to the long board and to each other as possible. Since your poles will retain some bends, there will have to be some small compromise in positioning the poles. You cannot simply press them together side by side.

Now, on the long board, start at the floor board and measure upward 12 inches. Place a mark at this point on the long board. Then 12 inches three times more. So that you end up with four marks, one foot apart on the long board.

With the aid of a try square or a combination square, carry these marks across four of the poles: two short ones and two long ones. Now, draw a second series of marks or lines exactly 1 inch above

All the legs are placed alongside one long straight board. The ends of the legs are kept in alignment by the small board at right angles to the long board. The small board is called the floor board. When you measure up on the long board and carry the measurements across the legs, the bends in the legs do not affect the measurements.

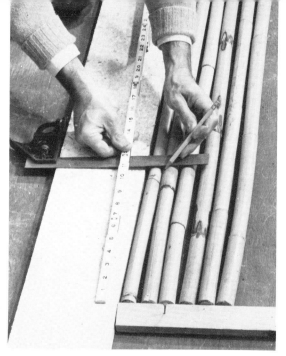

the first series of lines. With a pencil, darken the spaces between the lines where they fall on the four poles. This is the wood that will be removed when you cut the slots.

Return to the long board and repeat the measuring and marking operation. Start at the floor board and measure upward 12 inches. Then measure upward 18 inches three times again so that you have four pencil marks 18 inches apart.

Again, with the help of a try or combination square carry these four marks across the poles. *But do not mark the first two poles.* Just mark the four long poles.

Measure and draw a second series of lines exactly 1 inch above the first four lines. Again, *do not mark the short poles.* On the four long poles, darken the spaces between the parallel lines.

Cutting the rabbets   The shelves fit into rabbets cut into the poles. Rabbets are flat-bottomed grooves or slots. The two short poles only carry the ends of the short shelves. The two long poles that are positioned more or less in the center of the etagere carry both the short shelves and the long shelves. These two central poles have eight rabbets each. The last two long poles, like the short poles, have only four rabbets each.

Once you have cut a rabbet into a pole, it is difficult, but not impossible to replace the piece of wood. So be very careful to make no more rabbets than you need, and to position them correctly. That is why the spaces between the lines were darkened; doing this makes it easier to keep track of where the saw cuts have to be.

One way to keep the bottoms of each rabbet parallel with the others on the same pole is to cut them all at more or less the same time. Place one pole in the vise, marked side up. Position your hacksaw just within one line so that the cut removes the line. Hold the saw parallel to the floor and saw away until approximately ⅛ inch of saw blade is left outside the rattan. At this instant the blade will have cut approximately ⅜ inch into the wood, which is what we want.

Next, place the saw blade just within the second mark. Hold the saw parallel to the floor and, of course, at right angles to the pole. Cut as deeply as before. Remove the piece of wood from between the cuts with a chisel or an old screwdriver used as a chisel.

The width of the slot you will make by positioning the saw blade this way will be about right for the thickness of the shelf board and the layer of burlap. If you plan to use cane webbing in place of the burlap, place the saw on top of the 1-inch-apart lines. Bear in mind that you do not want a tight fit here, either with the burlap or the cane, because if you have to force the shelf into place, the glued-on material will be torn loose and wrinkled.

Now you have made one rabbet. Move down the pole and do the rest. Should you find that you cannot hold the pole steady while you hack away at it with the saw, draw a line along the surface of the entire pole, being careful to keep it on the same plane for its entire length. Then move the pole in the vise as necessary. So long as this line is uppermost and you hold the hacksaw parallel to the floor, all your rabbets will have reasonably parallel bottom surfaces.

Cut all the rabbets taking care, as previously forewarned, that you are cutting the rabbets in the right place, on the right pole and that all of the rabbets are on the same side of the pole, one directly above the other. This sounds obvious on paper, but, believe this craftsman, it is easy to become confused in this matter.

ASSEMBLY
Fastening one pair of poles at a time

Place one long four-slot pole on your workboard, slots up, alongside the guide board. Place one eight-slot pole on the workboard, parallel to the first pole and about two feet or so away.

Slip the long shelves into the slots. The burlap on the three lower shelves must face upward, the burlap on the top shelf faces down. Fold the burlap out of the way as you fit the edges of the shelves into the slots. Position the end of each shelf about ¼ inch shy of the side of the pole. In other words, the pole forms the outermost edges of the étagère.

Use right-angle supports to hold the shelves vertical as you work. (One or two of them will do the job, since the poles hold the shelves parallel.)

Next, position the second long four-slot pole above the other four-slot pole. Press the pole down so that its slots go over the edges of the shelves. Position this pole so that it too projects a fraction of an inch beyond the ends of the shelves. Drill and counter-sink the pole for 1½-inch #8 screws. Drill your holes at an angle into the chipboard. If you drive the screws straight down and near the edge of the chipboard it may crack. Drive the four screws home.

Next, position the second eight-slot pole, slots down and in line with the first eight-slot pole. Fasten it in place with the same size wood screws.

Two long shelves have been slipped into their respective slots. Two right-angle supports hold the shelves perfectly vertical. Now the corner pole is being drilled for screws.

Now, since we have our partially assembled étagère lying conveniently on our workboard, we will trim the upper edges of the long shelves. This is not the only way to proceed with this job, but it is convenient.

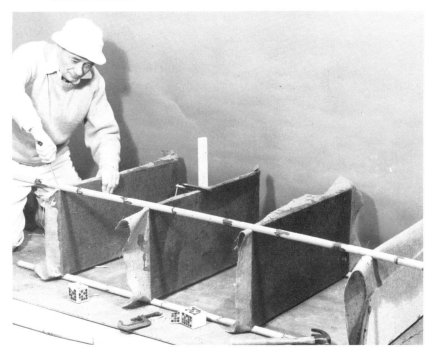

The partially assembled étagère has been turned around for the benefit of the photographer. Screws are being driven through the corner pole and into the shelves. Note the angle of the screw being driven. Note that the burlap on the top shelf is on the reverse side of all the other shelves.

Making and fastening some of the trim

All the shelf edges are trimmed, meaning that they are covered with ¾-inch rattan split in half, the flat side naturally going against the shelf edge.

Now all rattan will not split evenly, so start by figuring that you will lose about one pole in three. To cut your losses, examine the outside surface of the poles. If the grain or what appears to be the grain on the surface of a pole runs fairly evenly for the length of the pole, that pole should split fairly well.

Also, to reduce waste, cut the poles to be used for the long edges first. Then, if you cannot use the entire piece of rattan, you sometimes can use enough of it to cover a short edge.

Right now we are going to trim the edges of the four long shelves standing on edge on the workboard. The procedure is simple enough: Cut the ¾-inch pole ½ inch longer than the exposed edge of the shelf. Split the pole down the middle. A dull kitchen knife seems to work best. With your razor knife remove all the hairs and slivers from the split pieces of rattan. (While the split pieces may not be even, exact evenness is not necessary. The rattan does split quite easily and relatively evenly if you are careful.)

Fit the trim to the shelf edge. Cut the ends of the trim as necessary to fit neatly in place. Align the lower edge of the trim with the lower edge (when the étagère is standing up) of the shelf. Doing so will or may leave a narrow strip of burlap exposed. This is fine. The result is a better appearance than if the rather rough edge of the trim covered all of the burlap and edge of the shelf.

Nail the trim in place with 1¼-inch #16 wire brads. Three or four brads to one piece of trim are plenty. Keep away from the end of the trim; the brads will split it. And start your nailing near one end of the trim and work along the piece. If you nail near the ends first and then the center, you may end up with a bulge.

At this point you have fastened two split poles to the sides of the four long shelves. Though it may appear only natural to turn the shelves over and fasten the two poles now on the bottom, It is best not to try this. The shelves will flop down as you try to lift the partially assembled étagère and very possibly the shelves will pull loose and be damaged. Instead, install some of the braces that are needed.

Fasten the trim in place. Three or four brads are all that are needed. More may split the rattan.

Making the right-angle braces

As illustrated, the étagère has thirteen right-angle braces made from ¾-inch rattan. These are easy to make and install. The best way to make them is to make them all at one time. (You can, of course, use more if you wish.)

Cut the rattan into 18-or-so-inch pieces. Mark the center of each piece with a pencil mark. Place one piece of rattan in the vise in a vertical position, with about 4 inches of the pole within the vise jaws. Slip a length of pipe over the upper 4 inches of the vertical pole. Apply pressure, water, and heat. Keep your eye on the pole and on the center mark. When you think you have sufficiently overbent the rattan for it to return to the desired right angle, let go and watch the pole against any horizontal marker. In this way you do not have to remove the rattan from the vise to check the bend. If the rattan assumes a final angle of less than 90 degrees, meaning that the bend is sharper than a right angle, fine. Let it be. It is easy to open an angle. For some reason, once rattan has been bent, it is easier to unbend it than to bend it further. If you do not have a perfect right angle, or the bend is more than 90 degrees, bend it a little more.

Next drill and countersink two holes in each end of each brace. Keep the holes on the flat portion of the brace, and drill for 1¼-inch #8 screws.

Fasten right-angle braces to the lower long shelf. Note that the braces attach to the rattan on the side and are a small distance in from the edge of the shelf. This is done both for appearance and to keep the screws away from the edge of the shelf board.

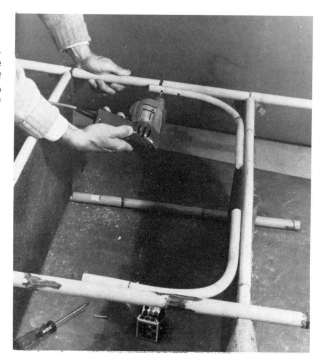

At this time all you need do is install the four braces that are fastened to the top side of the lowest long shelf and the underside of the top shelf—not to the shelf trim. (See the front view of the complete étagère.) There are, as stated, thirteen angle braces used, but you do not have to install them all now.

You can, if you now wish, trim the ends of the four long shelves.

Next the short shelves are fastened into place. Position one short pole on the workboard or the floor parallel to the eight-slot pole or leg now lying on the workboard. Next, slip the four short shelves into the appropriate slots in the two eight-slot middle poles. You now have one short four-slot pole or leg left. Position this, slots down, near the ends of the four short shelves. This helps hold them in line.

Align the short shelves with the two central legs (the eight-slot legs). Drill and countersink holes for 1½-inch #8 screws through the upper eight-slot leg into the short shelves. Drive the screws home. Align the fourth top leg with the ends of the short shelves. Drill and fasten as before.

Now, if you wish, you can trim the balance of the shelf edges that are easy to reach. At the same time you can remove the excess burlap with a razor knife. Final burlap cleaning is probably best done after everything else is completed and the étagère is erect.

Next, if you have no one to help you turn the étagère over, you can install one or more of the arch braces to help keep the shelves in place as you lift the piece of furniture. If you can secure help, you can install the arch braces later on; it is much easier that way.

The short shelves are slipped into the slots in the facing eight-slot legs. The ends of the long shelves have been trimmed.

The upper, center pole is drilled and countersunk. Then the ends of the short shelves are fastened with 1½-inch screws.

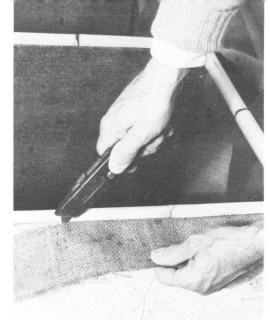

Next the end pole is fastened to the ends of the short shelves. Note that all the burlap on the short shelves is on top of the shelves.

The excess burlap can now be cutt off with a razor knife.

Installing the rest of the right-angle braces

Most of the give or bending in the étagère takes place at the legs beneath the lower shelves. That is why these legs must be braced in three or more directions. That is why eleven right-angle braces are used on the lower legs. More will do no harm. But less presents the possibility that the legs will break off when you lift the etagere. (This might happen if all the étagère's weight were to rest on one leg.)

Two more right-angle braces go at the rear of the lowest long shelf. No right-angle braces are used above the lowest of the four short shelves.

A right-angle brace is being fastened to one of the bottom shelves. Note how one brace end has been brought inside the other.

Close-up of the right angle braces at the short-shelf end of the bottom of the étagère.

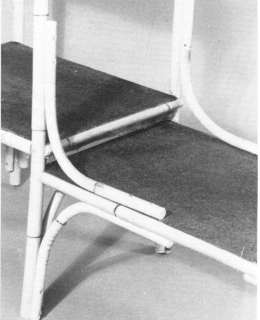

Making and installing the arch braces

Five arch braces of ¾-inch rattan are used. Two of these serve in part as ornamentation. The three that fit into the ends of the étagère are 14¾ by 16 inches overall. In other words, if you wish to draw a pattern, start with a rectangle this size and sketch an arc at one end. Or, since the arc is not critical, bend it by eye and check it against the actual opening as you work.

The ornamental arches go above the small shelves. Each arch brace is 16½ inches wide by 13½ inches high, made from a piece that is 35 inches long.

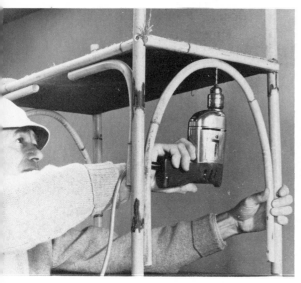

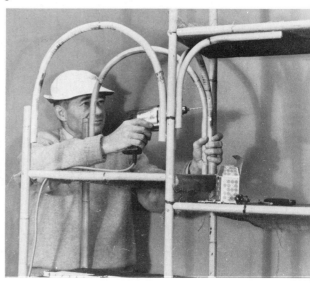

An arch brace is installed beneath the top long shelf end. A second arch brace goes beneath the other end of the same shelf. The third arch brace is at the bottom shelf directly in line with the brace shown.

The ornamental arch braces are fastened.

Installing the top crossbars

To finish the top of the étagère, three 1-inch rattan bars or short poles are used. Each is 15½ inches long. One is fastened to the top of the short poles, alongside the arch braces. The other two are fastened to the tops of the long poles, and they also run front to back.

FINISHING UP

Clean up all the cut ends with a little elbow grease and sandpaper. Then seal all the cut ends and all the bends that have lost silicon with clear enamel or a similar finish.

This done, cut all the excess burlap away. If you have difficulty with fraying ends, spray the burlap with enamel, let it dry, and then try cutting. The enamel or whatever will stiffen it so it can be easily cut and will not fray.

Next, paint all the burlap surfaces with clear enamel or a similar clear finish. Spray will do just as good a job, but it is far too costly. Give the first coat several days to dry really hard. Then go over the surface of the burlap with a little fine sandpaper. Blow the dust away and give the burlap several more coats of clear enamel, letting each coat dry before continuing.

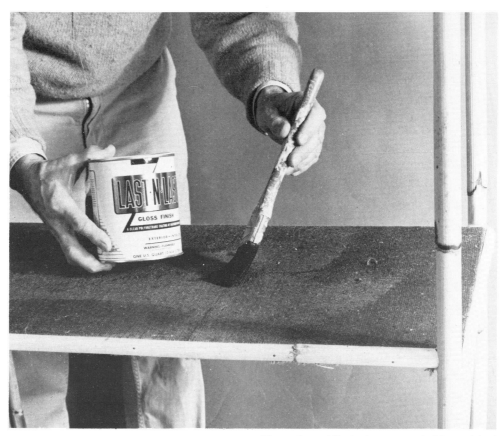

The surface of the burlap on one shelf is varnished.

Now, with your screwdriver, go over all the screws. For some reason or other they loosen after a few days, or maybe when you first tighten them, they heat up and so cannot be driven home.

Finish up by covering all the countersunk screw heads with a little putty that has been lightly colored with ocher.

14
CHAISE LONGUE

PARTS LIST	Side rails	2 pieces 1+-inch rattan pole, 72 inches long
	Legs (braces)	2 pieces 1-inch rattan pole, 31 inches long
		2 pieces 1-inch rattan pole, 20 inches long
		2 pieces 1-inch rattan pole, 48 inches long
	Third poles	2 pieces ¾-inch rattan pole, 48 inches long
	Crossbars	5 pieces 1-inch rattan pole, 18 inches long
		2 pieces 1-inch rattan pole, 19 inches long
		2 pieces 1⅜-inch rattan pole, 20½ inches long
	Straight braces	2 pieces 1-inch rattan pole, 19½ inches long
		2 pieces 1-inch rattan pole, 29 inches long
		1 piece 1-inch rattan pole, 23 inches long
		1 piece 1-inch rattan pole, 24 inches long
	Woods screws	1 box 1½-inch #8 flathead

The chaise pictured has been designed for indoor and outdoor service. It will stand up well to the weather if its feet remain dry. On a patio that is well drained, an occasional rain will do no harm. But if the chaise is permitted to stand on the grass, rot will soon creep up its legs and discolor the wood, eventually rotting it completely.

The cushion, or pad, shown is an outdoor pad in the sense it is water repellent. It can, of course, also be used indoors, but in a formal bedroom a single-color pad would probably be more appropriate.

The chaise is 64 inches long overall, 20½ inches wide, and 28½ inches high at its highest point. The cushion used is 2½ inches thick (on the average), 23½ inches wide, and 68½ inches long. The cushion overhangs the width of the chaise by an inch or more at each side, depending on the weight of the person resting on it. This helps keep the cushion from sliding off to one side, or falling between the frame sides. The ends of the cushion are a bit short of the ends of the chaise. The original design called for the chaise length to be somewhat less than that of the cushion. To make certain the side poles would be long enough, poles longer than necessary were bent. The finished product looked so good a bit longer than the cushion that that was the way the poles were left.

The completed chaise frame is very light. It weighs even less than the cushion. However, the chaise will easily hold a three hundred-pound man or woman, so long as he or she does not jump up and down on it.

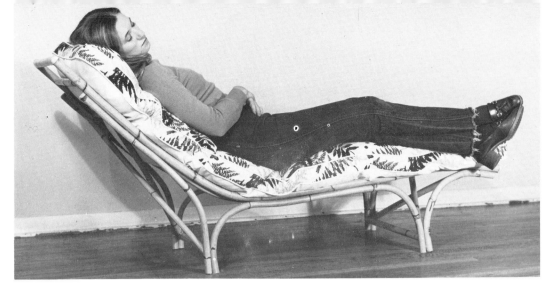

DESIGN VARIATIONS   This design was scaled to fit the cushion described. If you have or care to use a cushion of a different size, simply change the dimensions to fit.

The position of the legs in this design are not critical, but the rear legs must go behind the pivot point, which is where the rump goes and is the lowest point of the chaise's supporting frame. If you bring the legs forward, you might tip the chaise backward if you swing backward too quickly.

The legs are a combination of braces joined so as to work as legs also. You can reinforce the legs by adding vertical pieces behind them, but such reinforcement is unnecessary unless you expect to place much more than 300 pounds on the chaise.

Should you wish to stiffen the entire unit and remove some of the spring that is present — and that makes the chair more comfortable — join the legs with straight bars of ¾-inch rattan.

As designed, the angle of the chaise back is suitable for sleeping and reading. If you want a steeper angle, you must position the rear legs closer to the rear of the chaise.

The chaise frame alone.

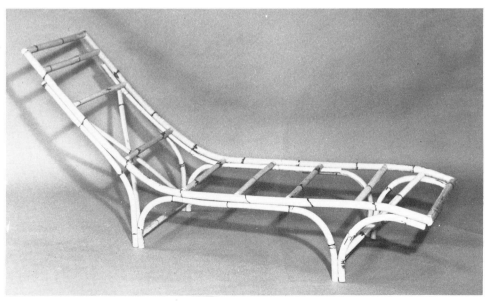

MAKING THE FRAME SIDES

Assuming that you are going with the dimensions given, start by drawing a rectangle on your workboard that is 64 inches long and 28½ inches wide. You don't have to draw the entire rectangle if you don't want to; three sides will do. Fasten a long straight board flush with one long side of the rectangle. So far as we are concerned from here on out, this board's edge represents the floor and we will build our frame on top of this "floor."

Next draw with chalk the outline of the frame as shown. The rear legs touch the "floor" 20 inches in from the rear end (high end) of the frame. The front legs touch the "floor" 13 inches back from the front end of the frame. The top surface of the low point of the frame is 10½ inches high (from the "floor") and is 26 inches from the rear end of the frame. The high point near the front of the frame is 12½ inches high and 8 inches back. If you mark these points on your workboard, you can sketch the curves in. They are not at all critical; neither are the dimensions — an inch or two either way will make little difference.

Sketch the full-scale outline for the side of the chaise. The long board represents the floor, on which the chaise will eventually rest.

Making the main frame members

These are the pieces of rattan that run the length of both sides of the chaise. They should be 1¼ inches thick, but 1-inch stock will do almost as well. It is best that these pieces not be spliced, but if you must, make each splice a long-step splice and position it clear of the bends.

Start with a pole 72 or more inches long. Bend the little curve up front first. Then bend the deeper curve. Take care that you do not introduce any side bends as you work. Your side rail, as we shall call this bent pole, must lie almost perfectly flat.

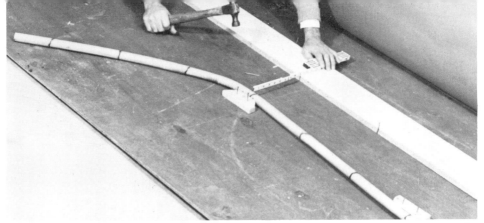

The side rail has been bent to shape. Here it has been placed atop the drawing. The point being measured should be 10½ inches from the "floor."

When you have completed your bending operations, place the bent pole on the board, positioning it on top of your sketch. If necessary, shift the pole a bit so that its distance from the floor board is close to the suggested distances. If necessary, bend some more or alter the dimensions.

This done, fasten guide boards to either side of the bent pole. These guides will be used as a gauge when you bend the second side rail.

Next, bend the rear half of the rear leg. This is made of 1-inch pole 31 inches long. When you have bent it, position one end against the "floor" board. Place the other end adjoining the rear portion of the side rail. The leg should touch the "floor" board the stated 20 inches from the rear of the chaise. Remember, we find the 20 inches by measuring straight down (to the "floor" board) from the top rear end of the chaise, then measuring 20 inches forward. The distance this rear leg runs up the back of the side rail pole is unimportant, just so long as it goes most of the way. It serves as a brace.

The next step is to bend the front half of the front leg. This too is made from 1-inch stock. Start with a 20-inch or longer pole. Bend it into a slightly sharper than 90-degree arc. Then try it against the side rail. You will have to cut it to make it fit. When you cut, make the front end a bit short of the front end of the side rail. Make the other end flush with the "floor" board.

The rear leg is being tried for fit. The chalk mark against the "floor" board is 20 inches in from the end of the chaise. This leg fits fairly well.

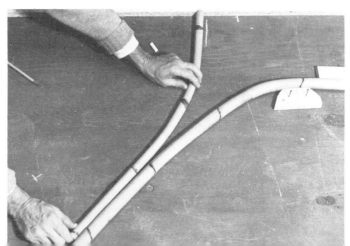

Bending the central arch brace

Remove the guide blocks under the side rail. At this juncture you have the front and rear halves of the front and rear legs in position on your workboard. They are not fastened down or to anything else, as yet. If you look, you will see that the "floor" board, the side rail and the legs form the guide necessary for your arch brace. In other words, your arch brace must fit between these frame members fairly closely. The closer the better.

The arch brace is strongest if it's made of one piece, but if you believe it will be too difficult, make two braces a little longer than necessary and then cut their ends so they fit.

For a single brace you need a 48-inch piece of 1-inch rattan. For two braces you will need a little more pole to start with. If you have spliced your side rail, keep the meeting point between the two braces at least 1 foot away from the side rail splice.

After you have bent and cut your central arch brace or braces to fit, position guide blocks on either side.

Guide blocks are being placed around the legs and central arch brace. The ends of these pieces have to be sawed flush with the "floor" board.

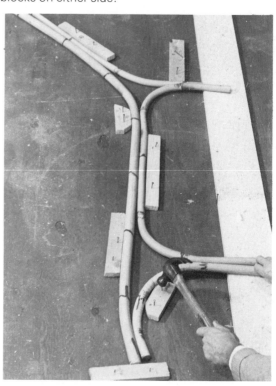

Assembling the frame side

Drill and countersink the braces for 1½-inch #8 wood screws. Start at any point that the brace meets and touches another brace and or the side rail. Fasten the two pieces together with a single screw driven through the brace and into the side rail at that point. Then, if necessary, you can bend the brace to conform to the side rail. Or, you can pull the two together with screws.

To finish, use two screws each and every place a brace touches another brace. Use two screws where the front leg contacts the side rail, four screws between the center of the arch brace and the side rail, and three or fourscrews between the rear leg and the side rail.

Now, build a second frame side as close to identical to the first as you can.

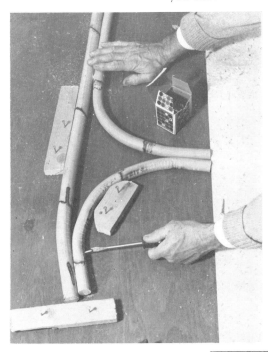 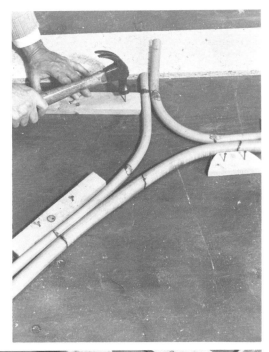

ABOVE LEFT: The legs have been cut to fit. Now the front leg, which is really a simple right-angle bend, is being screwed fast to the side rail.

ABOVE RIGHT: A block is placed alongside the rear leg. This end of the central arch brace has to be cut to match the rear leg.

RIGHT: The rear leg is fastened to the side rail. The slight bend remaining—beneath the hand—will be pulled up by the screws.

BOTTOM: One side frame completed.

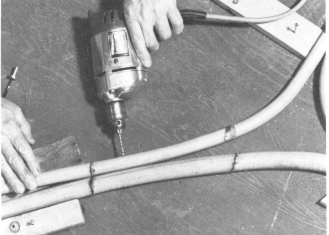

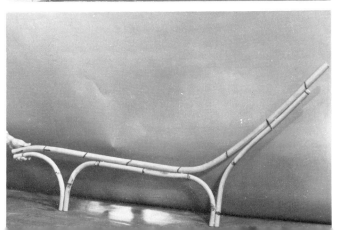

BRACING THE FRAME SIDES   A length of ¾-inch rattan, the "third pole," is fastened to the inner side of each frame between the braces and the side rail. When these third poles are fastened in place, they will make, with the side rails and braces, three-pole-diameter girders that are very strong and stiff. Each ¾-inch pole starts a few inches below the top of the rear leg and runs all the way forward to a point about 18 inches short of the front end of the chaise. You can make this pole longer if you wish. Again, it is best if it is a single piece, but if you have to splice it, just keep the splice a foot or so away from any splice in the side rail.

Each ¾-inch third pole needs to be about 48 inches long. All it requires is one bend that conforms to the central, large bend on the side rail.

Start fastening the third pole with 1½-inch screws near one end. Install screws every 10 inches or so. Drive one screw into the side rail, the next into the nearest brace, and so on.

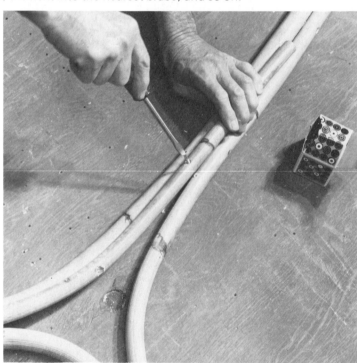

The third pole has been placed in position between the legs and central arch brace. Now it is being fastened into place with screws.

JOINING THE SIDES   Hold one frame side erect with the help of a right-angle support and clamp. Nail small blocks of wood—cleats—onto the workboard and around the legs of the frame so that it must remain vertical and cannot move. Then position the second side frame exactly parallel to the first, there should be exactly 18 inches from the inside of one frame to the next. Position cleats around the legs of the second frame so that it too cannot move.

This chaise has nine crossbars. Five crossbars are 18 inches long and rest on the third pole. Two bars are 19 inches long. Their ends are chamfered and they fit between the side rails; they are held in place by screws driven through the side rails. Two bars are fastened across the ends of the chaise. They are 20½ inches long. Use these numbers as general guides only. Your chaise will vary a little, and to secure a good fit, it is wise to measure the space each bar must fit. All the bars except the two end bars are cut from 1-inch stock.

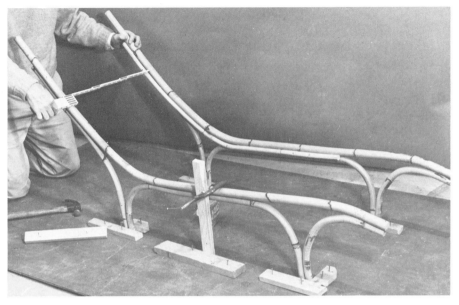

Both frame sides have been completed. Now they have to be joined by the crossbars and braces. Here, one frame is locked in position by cleats around its legs and held upright with aid of a right-angle support and cleat. The second side frame is being properly spaced from the first.

Installing the crossbars

Let us work with the five bars that rest on the third poles first. The first bar is positioned approximately 11½ inches down from the end of the chaise. The next bar is positioned 11 inches further away. The next is 10 inches away, and the following two bars are 8½ and 8 inches away respectively.

Cut each bar to fit the allotted space between the side rails. Place each bar in position, its ends atop the third poles. If the crossbar projects above the side rail, cut some of the underside of the crossbar's end away. Fasten the bars to the third pole with 1½-inch screws.

A crossbar is installed resting on the third pole. The combination square is used to hold the bar at a right angle to the side rail.

Next, install the crossbars that fit between the side rails and do not rest on the third poles. One goes about 4 inches down from the back end of the chaise. The other goes about 11 inches in from the front and low end of the chaise. Both bars are held in place by 1½-inch screws driven through the side rails.

None of the spacing dimensions are anything near critical. Bar position has been selected to place the bars where the maximum weight is expected. But do take care to fit the bars accurately, and for appearance's sake, place them at right angles to the side rails.

The end bars on the chaise shown are made of 1⅜-inch stock. The thicker material makes for a slightly better appearance. Each bar is cut just as long as the outside dimension of the chaise. In this case 20½ inches long. Then a step 1 inch deep and 1 inch wide was cut on each end of the crossbar. In this way the ends of the crossbar partially cover the ends of the side rails. One-and-a-half-inch screws driven through the end bars into the side rails hold the end bars in place.

Installing the straight braces

We have mentioned that the legs act as braces in addition to acting as legs. The braces now to be discussed are additional braces made of straight 1-inch rattan.

Start by chamfering both ends of a 19½-inch-long 1-inch pole to fit between the front legs of the chaise. Drill the legs and fasten this brace between the two legs, parallel to the surface of the floor and about 1½ inches clear of the floor.

Next, measure from the juncture between this horizontal brace and the leg to a point 3 inches in from the end crossbar on the top rail opposite. The distance will be less than 23 inches or so—this is the length of the 1-inch bar you will need for the brace. Next, measure from the other end of the horizontal brace up to the first side rail. The distance will be less than 24 inches, but you should start with a brace this long.

Shape the end of one brace to fit snugly between the horizontal brace and the leg. Shape its other end to rest smoothly between the third pole and the side rail. Join the ends of this diagonal brace to the legs and rail with 1½-inch screws. Do the same with the other diagonal brace. Then join the braces where they cross and touch each other with a wood screw. You will find that the slight give in each pole allows them to cross each other without difficulty.

The same is done at the rear legs. A 19½-inch-long horizontal brace is installed a short distance above the floor. Then a diagonal brace is installed that runs from the horizontal brace and leg as far up the side rail as the end of the third pole. The brace is screwed fast to the underside of the third pole. A second brace is installed in an opposite direction, and the two braces are joined by a screw. All of these braces are made of 1-inch stock and each of the diagonals is 29 inches long before its ends are cut to fit.

The lower end of the front diagonal brace is fastened to the juncture of the horizontal brace and leg. Note the piece of wood or cleat holding the front leg in position.

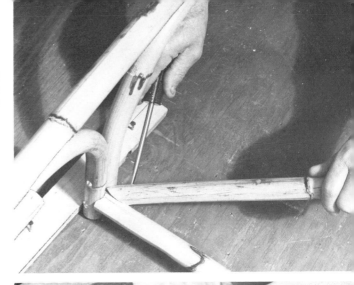

The top of one of the front diagonal braces is fastened to the third pole at the front of the chaise.

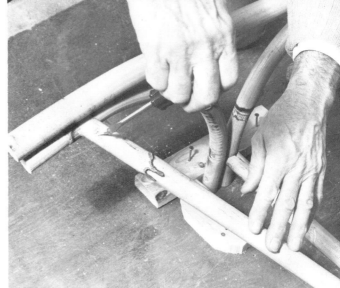

BELOW LEFT: One of the rear cross braces is fastened to the bottom of the third pole near the end of the chaise. Note the horizontal brace between the rear legs.

BELOW RIGHT: A hole is being drilled in one of the crossbars that rest on the third pole. Note how the front diagonal braces are installed. Note also the front crossbar joint detail.

FINISHING UP   With sandpaper clean up and smoothen all the sawed pole ends. Fill the screw holes and any holes you may have made in error with putty lightly colored with ocher. Seal the cut ends of the rattan, and with any clear enamel or varnish, seal the sides of the rattan where the silicon has been pried loose by bending, and you're done.

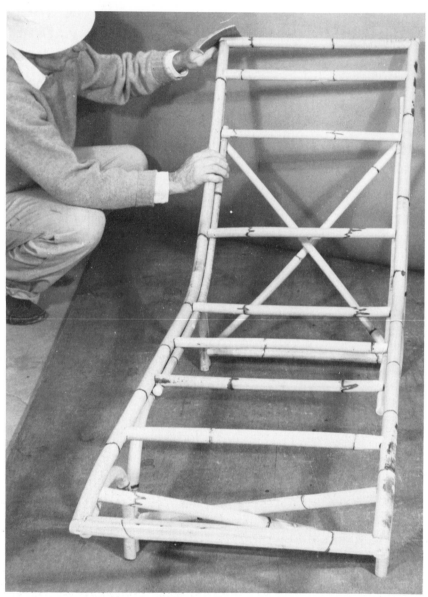

Front view of the completed chaise. All that needs to be done is a little sandpapering.

15
TEA CART

PARTS LIST		
	Shelves	2 pieces ¼-inch glass plate, 13½ by 24 inches
	Casters	4 2-inch wheel
	Legs	2 pieces 1¼-inch rattan pole, 24 inches long
		2 pieces 1¼-inch rattan pole, 38 inches long
	Shelf frames	4 pieces ¾-inch rattan pole, 13 inches long
		4 pieces ¾-inch rattan pole, 24 inches long
	Handle	1 piece ¼-inch rattan pole, 16 inches long
	Horseshoe braces	2 pieces ¾-inch rattan pole, 60 inches long
	Right-angle braces	4 pieces ¾-inch rattan pole, 14 inches long
	Guardrails	2 pieces ¾-inch rattan pole, 24 inches long
	Wood screws	40 1¼-inch #8 flathead
		2 1½-inch #8 flathead
		8 1-inch #7 flathead

The tea cart pictured being used as a flower cart is 34½ inches high, 16 inches wide, and 31½ inches long overall. The pieces of glass utilized as the supporting surfaces are 13½ inches wide and 24 inches long. Quarter-inch plate glass is used, but you can get by with double-weight window glass if you have a gentle hand pouring tea. The caster wheels are 2 inches high. The wheel support lifts the bottom of the cart legs another ⅜ inch.

End view of cart, glass not in place.

DESIGN VARIATIONS   There are a number of different ways you can construct the same basic wagon. Should you want to use the cart as an adjunct to your dining table, let us say as a serving cart, the cart could be made a few inches taller and even larger. Or you could use much larger casters.

If you are pressed for space, the curve on the handles could be made shorter or omitted, and the handle could be positioned on top of slightly taller end poles.

As an alternative to the glass supports you could use chipboard covered with webbed cane or varnished burlap. And, to reduce the chance of window glass supports breaking, you could include a number of crossbars beneath the glass.

In place of the straight guardrails positioned parallel to the glass, you could build an ornamental wall or border of thin rattan curved into a wave shape or a series of circles.

Another variation you may have seen elsewhere utilizes only two wheels. These are under the front legs. The rear legs rest on the floor. To move this cart the rear legs are lifted up a little. The advantage of this design is that the cart cannot be accidentally pushed and moved. Should you opt for this variation, be certain to use large front wheels for the sake of appearance.

MAKING THE LEGS   All four legs are made of 1¼-inch poles. The front legs are 24 inches long. The rear legs—the legs that also carry the handle—are 35 inches long, but it is wiser to start with 38-inch poles and then cut them to suit after bending.

To bend the legs place 4 inches of the pole between the vise jaws and try for as close—small radius—a bend as you can. If you want to draw a rectangle on your workboard as a guide, make it 6 by 32½ inches and fit the leg inside. In any event the bend is not critical at all, but you should try to make both bends as alike as possible.

Next, chamfer the tops of the bent ends of the rear legs. Make the chamfer suitable to accept an 1¼-inch pole, which of course will be the cart handle.

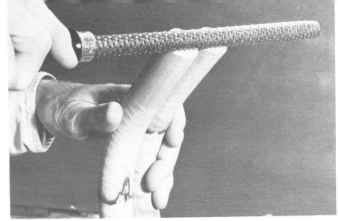

The top ends of the legs that carry the handle are chamfered.

Cutting and marking
Place one bent leg on top of the other. Align the curved portions of the legs, then mark and cut the ends of the legs to make them identical in length. Since no two rattan poles will ever bend exactly the same, you will find that to get the curves aligned, you will have to trim the pole ends individually.

Next we have to mark the position of the shelf frames on the legs. Since the legs are not perfectly straight, you cannot simply measure up from an end. You must allow for the bends.

Fasten one length of scrap lumber to your workboard. At the end of this piece of wood nail a second piece of scrap lumber to it and at right angles to it. Place the ends of one straight leg and one curved leg against the second piece of wood. Align the sides of the legs with the first piece of wood. Now the legs are parallel despite their bends. Now you can measure up on the first board and carry the mark across both legs.

Make one mark 5 inches up from the leg bottom. Make a second mark another 15 inches up (or 20 inches from the bottom). These marks indicate the upper surface of the shelf frames before the glass is installed.

Mark two legs at a time, bearing in mind that you must make the marks on the facing sides of the legs, because that is where the shelves will go — between the facing sides of these legs.

The legs are placed in a guide and marked. The purpose of the guide is to enable the craftsman to mark the correct shelf height on the legs despite the bends in the legs.

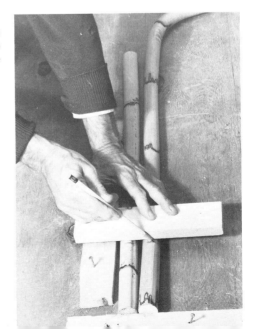

Installing the casters

Select a wood drill that will make a hole just a fraction larger than the hole required by the caster supports. Place the cart legs in your vise and drill into the leg ends to a depth equal to the support portion of the casters plus ¼ inch or so.

To install the casters, merely press them home into their holes. If you find the hole is too narrow, do not force the caster; you may split the pole. Redrill with a larger diameter bit. If you find the hole too large, wrap several layers of masking tape around the caster's end. That will make it snug. If at a later date you find the caster's support turning instead of the wheel, smear a little epoxy cement on top of the masking tape.

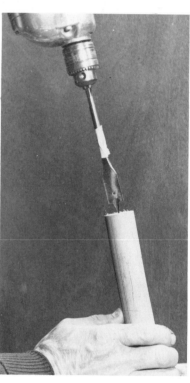

A hole is drilled in the end of a leg in order to receive a caster. The tape on the drill bit serves as a depth guide.

MAKING THE SHELF FRAMES

Both shelf frames are made from ¾-inch stock. Both frames are identical in size with outside dimensions of 14½ by 24 inches. The sides overlap the end pieces.

Start by drawing with chalk a rectangle on the workboard that is exactly 14¼ by 24 inches in size. Align four pieces of scrap lumber on the outside of the four lines. Nail these guide boards to the workboard. Your two shelf frames must fit within this area.

Cut four pieces of ¾-inch rattan pole exactly 24 inches long. Cut four more pieces of ¾-inch pole 13 inches long. Next, position two long poles within the outline. Chamfer the ends of two short poles until they can just fit between the two long poles.

Drill across the ends of the long poles and into the ends of the short poles. Countersink and join the poles with 1¼-inch #8 wood screws. Do this at all the four corners. When you have finished, you will have a rectangular frame that is perfectly flat and exactly 14¼ by 24 inches overall. Now make a second frame.

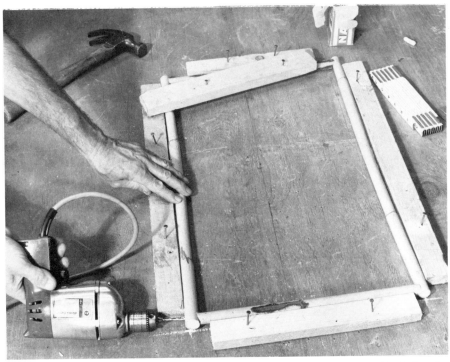

Scrap wood is used to form a guide around the rectangle drawn with chalk on the workboard. Each shelf must fit within this frame. Then the shelf frame is assembled. Note how the ends of the short pieces of pole have been chamfered to fit. A pilot hole is being drilled through one pole and into the end of another. A screw will later be used to hold the two pieces of rattan together.

ASSEMBLING THE CART

Next you must chamfer the legs, position the frames within the chamfers, and hold all the parts orthagonal — a fancy word meaning "square" — while you fasten them together with screws.

The easy way to do this, and that is the way we choose to do it, is to use a simple jig made of guide boards nailed to the workboard and a right-angle support. The arrangement is illustrated in an accompanying photograph.

Use guides to hold two legs in position. Then cut the chamfers across the two legs. Each chamfer, or groove, should be positioned immediately below and parallel to the marks previously made. Cut each chamfer about ¼ inch deep at this time.

Place one frame within a pair of grooves, held vertical to the legs with the aid of a right-angle support. Make the end of the frame flush with the side of the leg. Drill a hole through the frame and into the leg. Countersink the hole and insert a 1¼-inch screw to fasten the frame to the leg. Then fasten the second leg to the other end of the frame.

Next position the second frame within the second pair of grooves on the same leg, held perfectly vertical, and fasten with screws driven through the frame and into the legs.

Next place the second pair of legs on the workboard between the guides. Now position the first frame, attached to a pair of legs within the chamfers in the second pair of legs. Again use the right-angle support to hold the frame vertical and make the ends of the frame flush with the sides of the legs.

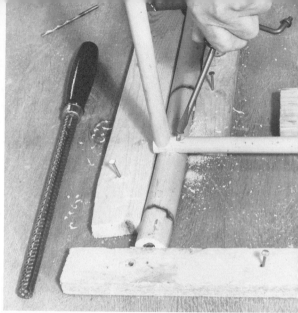

One short leg and one long leg have been chamfered and positioned within the guide—the poles parallel to each other and their ends aligned. The lower shelf frame is positioned and made vertical with the aid of the guide. Note that the frame end is being made flush with the side of the pole.

A pilot hole is first drilled through frame and into leg, then a screw is driven into the hole.

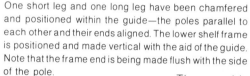

Then, position and fasten the second frame to the legs.

At this time it may be advisable to check the fit of the glass in the cart. Stand the cart on its legs and carefully lower the glass onto a frame. The glass should be shy of the insides of the poles by about $3/16$ inch on each side. If the distance is greater, you should increase the depths of the chamfers and you will need to disassemble the cart partially to do this. The deeper the chamfers, the stronger the joint. If there isn't at least $1/16$-inch clearance on both sides of the glass, you may have trouble inserting the glass. You can either replace the short sides or ends of the frames with slightly longer pieces of pole at this point, or else take your chances that you won't have to do this once the cart is completely assembled. (You can also cut the glass narrower, if you wish.)

LEFT: The second set of legs being attached to the lower shelf frame.

BELOW: The second shelf frame being attached to the legs.

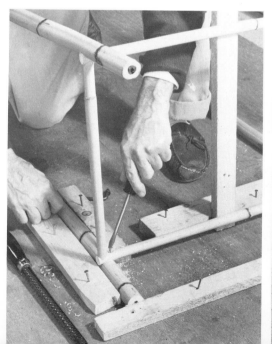

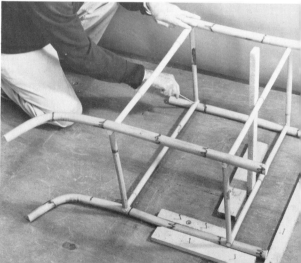

MAKING AND FASTENING THE HANDLE

The handle is made from a 16-inch piece of 1¼-inch pole — a thicker piece of pole would look even better. Both ends are rounded and made smooth. The handle is placed in position and drilled and countersunk for 1½-inch #8 screws. If the two leg arms are a bit out of line, now's your chance to straighten them up a little.

Before fastening the handle, double-check the chamfering; you want the fit here to be neat and close because these two joints are highly visible. After the screws are in, fill the holes with colored putty.

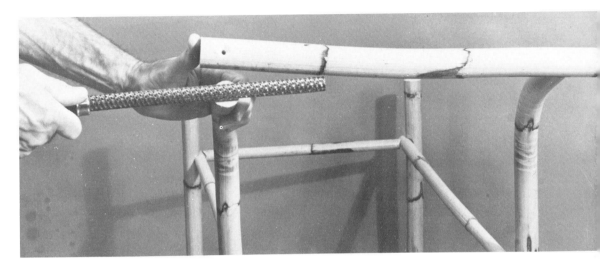

Final chamfering to fit handle closely to top of leg.

MAKING THE HORSESHOE BRACES

The horseshoe braces help hold the cart together, add a little charm, and also serve as the end walls or barriers for both shelves.

They are bent from ¾-inch rattan poles 60 inches long. You can use a slightly shorter piece of pole for each brace. It is not necessary that the brace ends go below the lower shelf, as is the case in the cart illustrated.

Start by drawing a rectangle in chalk on your workboard that is 15 by 19 inches in size. If you wish, you can draw the complete outline of the cart's end. Doing so will possibly give you a better perspective of the shape of the brace. Next sketch the desired brace curve. Make the curve the same size as the rectangle you have drawn or a little larger.

Fasten guides to the workboard, and then bend the poles to fit the guide. Bear in mind you cannot put any pressure on the braces when you attach them to the car. The braces must hold the cart orthogonal; if they are forced into shape on the cart, they will pull it out of line.

Bear in mind too that the two braces do not have to be exact duplicates of each other. As long as they are about the same size and have about the same curve, they will look fine.

To fasten a brace, place the cart on end. Place the braces on the cart without in any way pushing or pulling the braces to do so. Position the brace, and hold it in position with a clamp. Then drill, countersink, and lock the brace in place with 1¼-inch #8 screws. If the cart does not stand perfectly straight, you can use the end braces to straighten the cart up a little. But if the cart tilts badly, you should disassemble it and correct the error.

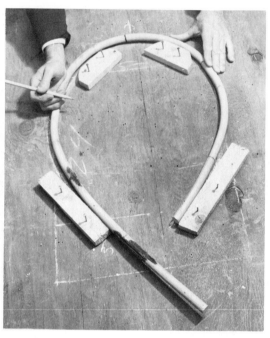

The rectangles drawn on the workboard represent the entire end of the tea cart. The lowest line represents the floor. The top line represents the upper guardbar or rail. Scraps of wood are nailed to the workboard to outline the horseshoe brace.

The imperfectly bent brace is fitted to the guide. The pencil is used to mark where bend changes are necesary. Extra pole length will later be cut off.

A horseshoe brace is clamped in position. The top of the brace will be fastened in place with screws. Then the lower portion can be pulled into correct alignment and screwed fast. The rigidity of the frame will keep it from being pulled out of line.

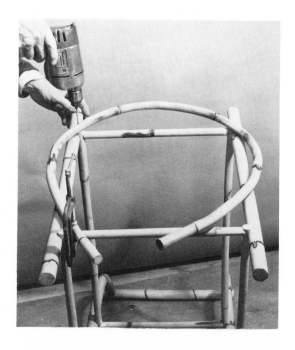

MAKING AND INSTALLING THE RIGHT-ANGLE BRACES

You need four of these braces in all. Each is made from ¾-inch rattan pole and each piece is 14 inches long before bending.

The easy way to make them is to make them all at the same time. Place 4 inches or more of one pole between the jaws of a vise. Wet and heat and bend with the help of a length of pipe. When you remove the pipe and release the bend, check by eye against a horizontal shelf or window ledge the angle at which the rattan stabilies itself. If the angle is a bit sharp, less than 90 degrees, fine. You can always open it a little when it is cold.

Drill and countersink each right-angle brace for two 1¼-inch #8 screws. Note that one end of the brace goes against the side of the leg, the other end of the brace goes against the *side* of the shelf frame, so the screw holes are not drilled in the same direction. Taper the ends of the braces and screw them in place.

A right-angle brace is bent. The portions of the pole in the pipe and below the vise jaws remain relatively straight.

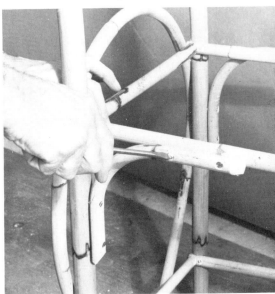

A right-angle brace is being fastened in place. Note where the screws are positioned.

MAKING THE GUARD RAILS

Each shelf has two guardrails along its long sides. Each rail is cut from ¾-inch rattan pole and is 24 inches long before final cutting and fitting.

The ends of each rail are chamfered at an angle so that the rail is not directly above the side of the shelf. This is done to permit the glass to be lowered onto the shelf. The guardrails are positioned 3½ inches above the side of the shelf below. Use 1-inch #7 screws to hold the guardrail in position.

FINISHING UP

Sand all the cut rattan pole ends and sand all the loose silicon free of the pole. Remove all the pencil marks, then seal the cut pole ends and the bare sections of the pole with a clear finish.

Lower the glass gently into place and you are ready to put the cart into service.

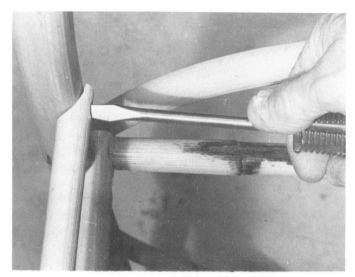

One end of a guardrail is fastened. Note how the end of the rail has been chamfered in order to allow the glass to be lowered onto the shelf.

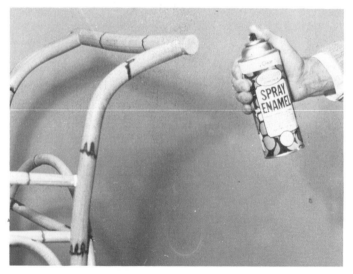

After all the rough ends have been sanded and all the holes plugged with colored putty, it is time to seal all the cut ends and bare-of-silicon places on the poles.

16
LOVE SEAT

PARTS LIST		
	Frame	2 pieces 1 + -inch rattan pole, 52½ inches long
		2 pieces 1 + -inch rattan pole, 18½ inches long
	Seat-slat supports	2 pieces ¾-inch rattan pole, 51 inches long
	Seat slats	10 pieces ¾-inch rattan pole, 16 inches long
	Legs	6 pieces 1-inch rattan pole, 13½ inches long
	Right-angle braces	8 pieces 1-inch rattan pole, 25 inches long
	Straight leg braces	2 pieces ¾-inch rattan pole, 18 inches long
	Arch braces	2 pieces ¾-inch rattan pole, 36 inches long
	Cross braces	2 pieces 1-inch rattan pole, 23 inches long
	Backrest supports	3 pieces 1¼-inch rattan pole, 30 inches long
	Backrest brace	1 1-inch rattan pole, 28 inches long
	Armrests	2 pieces 1 + -inch rattan pole, 48 inches long
	Curved end pieces	2 pieces ¾-inch rattan pole, 34 inches long
	Backrest top bar	1 piece 1-inch rattan pole, 57 inches long
	Backrest slats	10 pieces ¾-inch rattan pole, 16½ inches long
	Binding cane	
	Wood screws	1 box 1¼-inch #8 flathead*
		16 1½-inch #8 flathead
		12 2-inch #8 flathead
		12 2-inch #10 flathead
		30 1-inch #7 flathead

Screws by the box (100) will cost you far less than half the price of the same screws purchased by the dozen or plastic package.

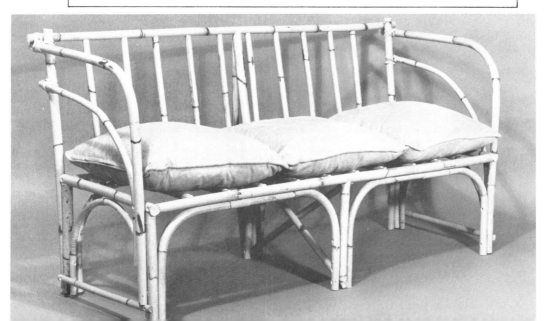

The love seat pictured can also be used as settee and as a medium-size sofa with arms and back. Just what the differences might be, if there are any, between these three pieces of furniture is beyond the scope of this book, but they are mentioned here just in case anyone asks, "Isn't that a settee you are building?"

As designed and described, the seat is 57 inches long, 29½ inches high, and 22 inches deep overall. It accommodates three 17- by 17-inch cushions and three ordinary individuals in a sitting position — or either one very short person or one large midget lying down.

DESIGN VARIATIONS   The basic design can be varied in size without structural changes. For example, the seat could be constructed as a couch by making it longer. In that case, two more pairs of legs would be added, plus a second reinforced or braced backrest support. (The backrest supports are the vertical pieces of rattan that connect the back of the seat to the lower portion of the frame.)

If you wanted to make the seat shorter so that it would only seat two individuals and hold two cushions, you would eliminate the central backrest support, but you would brace the end supports in the way the present center support is braced.

If you reduced the seat still further and made it suitable for one individual, everything would remain the same except that you would no longer need a central pair of legs and the backrest supports would not need to be braced. However, it would be advisable to go to an 18-inch-wide or slightly wider cushion for the single seater. Side arms on a seat that is only 17 inches wide are much too confining. "Chubbies" couldn't fit into it.

Eliminating the cushions   Seat height of the present design without seat cushions is only 13¾ inches. When 2½-inch-thick cushions are placed on top, seat height is increased to 16¼ inches, which is usual for a sofa and couch. So to eliminate the seat cushions, you would have to increase leg and leg brace heights accordingly, and you would have to at least double the number of seat slats presently used. There would be no need to change the number of back slats used, since no cushions have been planned for the backrest in the original seat.

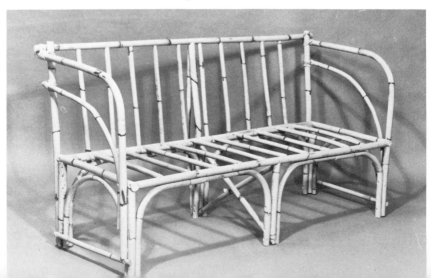

Adding cushions   If you wanted to add cushions to the backrest, you would have to increase the depth of the seat frame accordingly. If you wanted to add cushions to the insides of the armrests, you would have to increase the length of the frame accordingly.

CONSTRUCTING THE BASIC FRAME

This portion of the love seat is the rectangular frame that carries the seat slats and rests on the seat's legs. It is constructed of 1 + -inch poles at a minimum. You will need two poles 52½ inches long and two poles 18½ inches long.

Start by drawing a rectangle with chalk on the workboard. Make it exactly 18½ by 53½ inches in size. Outline three sides of the box with wood guides fastened to the workboard. Place the two short poles at the ends of the rectangle. The two long poles go between the short ones. Chamfer the pole ends to fit. Then drill through the short poles and into the ends of the long poles. Countersink the holes and then secure the joints with 1½-inch #8 screws.

This done, examine the frame. If it lies flat to within ¼ inch or so of the workboard, fine. Let it be. If not, disassemble the frame, bend the offending pole as needed, and reassemble.

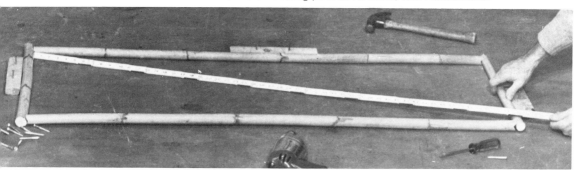

Building the basic frame. By measuring the diagonal of the rattan rectangle both ways, you can easily check it for squareness.

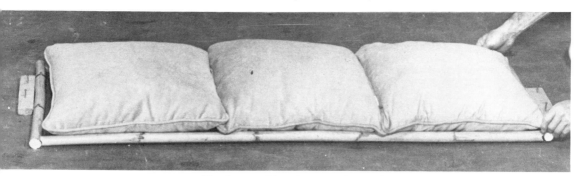

The three cushions that are to be used are placed on the basic frame in order to check its size.

Adding the seat slats

With the seat frame flat on the workboard, place two pieces of ¾-inch rattan, each 51 inches long, inside the frame and on the workboard. Push each piece against the side of the frame. Join each piece, which we shall call the seat-slat, or seat-bottom, support, to the frame with 1½-inch #8 screws placed about 8 inches apart.

The seat-bottom support is fastened to the inside of the basic frame with screws.

Next, cut some of your stock of ¾-inch poles into ten pieces, each 16 inches long. These will form the seat slats. Position the slats across the seat frame so that the ends of each slat rest on the ¾-inch-thick seat-bottom supports. Space the slats equidistant. You needn't be accurate here. Examine the ends of each slat in relation to the surface of the seat frame poles. If the tops of the slats are flush with the poles' surface, fine. If they protrude above the surface, cut the end of the slat so that it does become flush. Then drill through the slat ends into the support and join the slats to the support with 1-inch #7 screw.

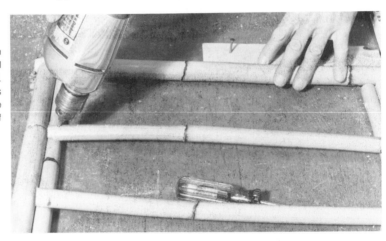

The seat slats are fastened with screws after pilot holes are drilled through slats and into support. Note how the ends of the slats have been cut to make their top surfaces flush with top surface of the basic frame.

COMPLETING THE SEAT

To ease the confusion that already exists in our workshop, let alone the world at large, we shall call that portion of the love seat upon which someone will sit, but minus the arms and back, the seat. At this point we have constructed the basic frame and have added the slats. Now we will complete the seat. This consists of adding the legs and braces.

Adding the legs

There are six legs in all — one at each corner and one in the middle of each long frame piece. Each is 13 inches long, but you would be wise to start with 13½-inch legs just in case your chamfering has to be redone and the frame poles are not quite 1¼ inches thick above the leg ends.

In any case, cut the legs from 1-inch or thicker stock. Chamfer one end of each to fit the frame it will contact and support. Place the frame on top of the legs. (It will be very helpful to find someone to hold the frame at this time.) Drill down through the frame and into the end of the leg. You will have to drill the hole to one side of the screw already in position in the frame at the corners. Countersink the hole and drive a screw partly into the leg. Inch-and-a-half #8's will do fine here. Do this on all the legs. Then place cleats on the workboard and around the legs to more or less hold them in place.

Next, use a try square or a combination square to make certain each leg is vertical. Adjust as may be needed, then drive the screws home.

The leg has been fastened to the basic frame with a wood screw that has been driven alongside the screw holding the frame together. Here the leg is made vertical in relation to the frame. Cleats or guides will hold it in place while the other legs are being fastened.

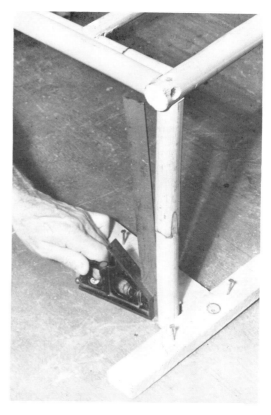

Adding the right-angle braces   There are eight of these braces and they are all made from 1-inch stock. Each brace is 25 inches long before bending and trimming — a little will have to be cut off after bending. Place 5 inches of the pole between the vise jaws when you start your bend. Place about 7 inches of the other end of the pole in a length of pipe. In this way you will secure two relatively flat sections on the end of the right-angle brace.

As stated several times before, do all the right-angle braces at one time. Judge the angle against a mark on the wall. It is fine if you end up with a sharper-than-90-degree angle. Then you can open the angle to fit perfectly. And in this case, we need perfect fits because it is the brace that holds the leg vertical.

Fasten one right-angle brace in place with four 1¼-inch #8 screws, taking great care to make certain the leg remains vertical. Then fit the adjoining brace in place. There will be an overlap of brace ends and you will have to cut the second brace's end a little. When you do, take care; it is easy to cut too much here. You want

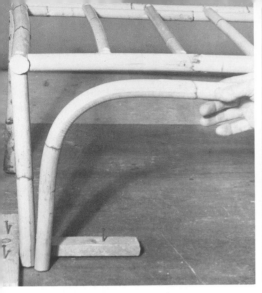

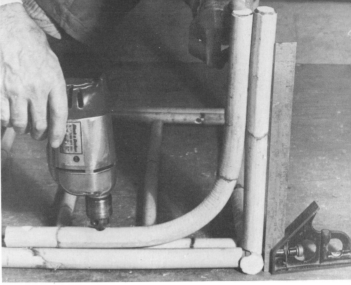

A right-angle brace is checked prior to fastening it with screws. Brace angle must be perfect, or the leg will be forced out of position.

Holes are drilled through the brace and into the seat frame. Use the combination square to make certain the leg remains vertical.

to end up with the brace ends touching or nearly touching.

Install four right-angle braces along the same side of the seat. Now you can install the balance of the right-angle braces along the other long side of the seat.

Adding the straight leg braces   Check to make certain two end legs are prefectly parallel and vertical. Fasten or lock them in this position by nailing a piece of scrap lumber across the leg ends.

Next fasten a straight piece of ¾-inch pole across the pair of legs. You will need a piece of rattan 18 inches long. Position it about 2½ inches below the ends of the legs, which are now in an upside-down position. Use 1½-inch #8 screws. We shall call this piece of rattan a straight leg brace. The piece of scrap lumber can now be removed. Repeat this procedure for the other pair of end legs.

A piece of scrap lumber is nailed across the ends of two legs. The scrap lumber holds the legs parallel. The straight leg brace is fastened to one leg. A rule is used to make certain the brace is horizontal before it is fastened with a wood screw.

Adding the arch braces   Now bend an arch brace to shape and fit it into the space between the legs and behind each of the straight leg braces.

Each arch brace is 36 inches long and cut from ¾-inch rattan. You can, if you wish, sketch the shape of the desired curve within a rectangle that is 16 inches long and 13 inches wide. Or you can just bend the pole by eye, fitting it into the required space as you go. Since the straight leg brace locks the legs in position, you do not require an accurate bend to the arch; you can snap it into place or spread it a little to make it fit. Use five or six 1¼-inch #8 screws to hold it in place. The ends of the arch, incidentally, need only go below the straight leg brace.

Cutting the legs to size   At this juncture you have installed all the right-angle braces, both arch braces, and both straight braces. Before going further, it may be advisable to turn the seat over and examine each leg and its adjoining braces. If any one is higher than the others, cut it down to the same height.

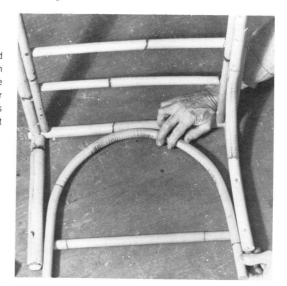

An arch brace is fitted into the space at one end of the love seat. Since the legs are locked in place by the straight brace, the arch brace curve need not be perfect. You can spread it or restrict the brace as required. The brace is fastened with screws to the legs and the seat frame.

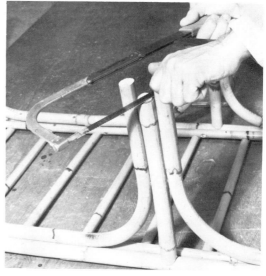

All the braces are cut flush with the ends of the legs.

Installing the cross braces

Go to either center leg. Remove one of the adjoining right-angle braces. Place the edge of the hacksaw on the side of the leg. Angle the blade toward the point where the opposite leg is joined to the seat frame. Position the high point of the blade so that it is about 1 inch below the top of the leg (the top of the leg — actually its lower end — is pointing skyward, since the seat is upside down). With the hacksaw in this position, cut diagonally across the leg and remove the angle-ended piece of leg.

One of the two right-angle braces connected to each center leg is removed. Then the leg is cut off at an angle at a distance of 1 inch from the end of the leg.

Next, position a 23-inch long piece of 1-inch rattan so that one end of the pole rests on top of the diagonal saw cut you have just made, and the other end rests alongside the juncture between the opposite leg and the frame. If a better fit can be secured, chamfer and/or cut the end of the cross brace that rests against the frame.

Drill and countersink the ends of the cross brace and fasten the brace to the leg end and the frame with 1½-inch #8 screws. Replace

One cross brace is installed. One end of the cross brace is fastened with a screw to the cut-off end of one middle-of-the seat leg. The other end of the cross brace is fastened alongside the other leg where it joins the seat frame.

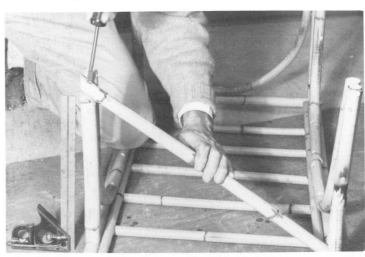

the right-angle brace. Trim the end of the cross brace if necessary.

Now install a second cross brace the same way. Join the two braces at the point of crossing with another 1½-inch #8 screw.

The seat or bench portion of the love seat is now completed. Should you wish to use it this way, finish it off as described before. Fill the holes with colored putty, sand the rough edges, and seal the raw edges and silicon-free surfaces with any kind of clear varnish or lacquer.

The second cross brace is installed diagonal to the first. Then the two braces are joined by means of a wood screw where they cross.

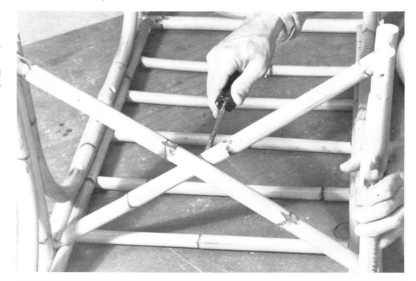

Here is the completed seat minus its sides and back, right side up.

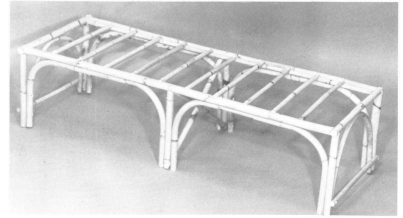

The same seat upside down. Note how the cross braces have been connected.

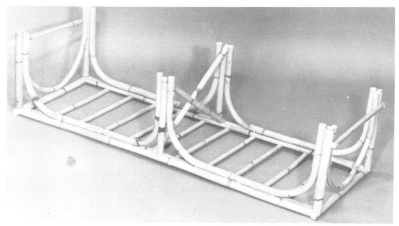

CONSTRUCTING AND ADDING THE BACKREST

The backrest consists of a number of slats supported by one long horizontal pole in turn supported by three vertical poles fastened to the rear legs of the seat.

Making the backrest supports

Each of the three backrest supports is a 1¼-inch-thick rattan pole 30 inches long before bending and a little cutting. If you do not use 1¼-inch poles for the supports, you must brace the two end supports just as the center support is now braced. (Support bracing is discussed shortly.)

Each backrest support has a single bend about 13 inches above its bottom end. To make this bend place 13 inches of pole in the vise and apply the heat just as closely to the top edge of the vise as you can. Make the bend or angle small to produce a displacement of about 2 inches at the top end. The only important thing about the bends on the supports is that they be identical. If they are not, the backrest will be crooked.

Fastening the backrest supports

Clamp a support to one seat leg. Make the bottom end of the support flush with the bottom of the leg. Position the support parallel to the leg and vertical to the floor, with the angle tilting away from the seat. Drill and countersink for three 2-inch #10 screws. The most important of these screws is the top one. That takes most of the load. Place that one as high as you can without the tightened screw pulling the support towards the leg. In other words, the position of the top screw should be just below the point where the support and leg separate. Do the two end supports now. Let the center support go till later.

Fasten a backrest support to the seat. Position the highest of the three screws you should use here as far up on the support as you can without bending the support.

Making and fastening the armrests

Each armrest is made from a 48-inch-long piece of 1 + - inch rattan. The single bend is made with a moderate radius and is not quite a right angle. The top of the armrest runs slightly uphill backward. The point at which it joins the support is about 1 inch higher than the point at which the armrest bends downward. If you want to bend the pole to a definite outline rather than bend it by eye alone, draw a rectangle on the workboard in chalk that is 28 by 23 inches in size. Draw an arc in one corner of the rectangle and then bend the pole to fit.

The high end of the armrest is attached to the back support at a point about 28 inches above the floor, as measured to the top surface of the pole. The other end of the arm rest is fastened to one side of a corner leg. The lower end of the armrest pole sits atop the straight leg brace.

One 2-inch #8 screw is used to fasten the armrest to the vertical backrest support. Two 1½-inch #8 screws are all that are needed to fasten the other end of the rest to the front leg.

An armrest is checked before being fastened. You want the rest to have a slight upward pitch as it approaches the backrest.

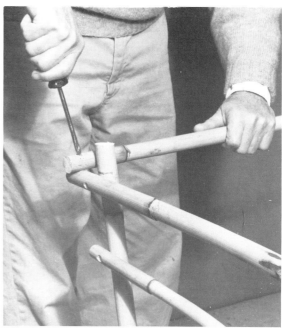

The armrest has been fastened to the backrest support In addition, the curved end piece has also been fastened in place. Now the backrest top bar is fastened to the armrest. A second screw should be driven through the top bar and into the backrest support, the vertical pole.

Making and fastening the curved end pieces

To fill the space beneath the armrests and to further brace the backrest, a curved end piece is used. Very simply, this is a 34-inch-long piece of ¾-inch rattan that is bent more or loss into a quarter circle. Its high end is screwed fast to the backrest support. Its low end is fastened alongside the lower end of the armrest. No special care is needed when making these two pieces. Judge the bends by eye, and make them both more or less alike.

Fastening the backrest top bar

This is a 1-inch pole, 57 inches long. It rests on top of the ends of the armrests and behind the end backrest supports. It is fastened in place by two, 2-inch #8 screws. One screw is driven into the armrest; the other goes through the backrest bar and into the support.

Installing and bracing the center backrest support

This support is bent to the same angle as the others. Its top end, however, does not rest against the backrest top bar. Instead, its end is cut and chamfered to fit beneath the backrest top bar. A single 1½-inch #8 screw down through the top bar is all that is needed to fasten the top of the support to the bar resting on it.

The brace is made from a 28-inch-long piece of 1-inch stock. This pole is bent in the middle so that when it is laid lengthwise on top of the central backrest support, a space of about 4 or 5 inches exists in the middle between the two pieces of rattan. Then the ends of the brace are cut with a saw and filed down to a long angle so that there is 2 or 3 inches of each end that can be made to lie flat against the backrest support. Now, all you need do is fasten the brace to the support with six wood screws driven through the tapered portions of the brace. Use 1¼-inch #8 screws.

The third and middle backrest support is now installed. Note that the top of this bar is chamfered to fit beneath the backrest top bar.

The middle back-rest support is braced. This brace is merely a slightly bent piece of 1-inch rattan, its ends tapered to fit the adjoining pole and held in place by three screws at each end.

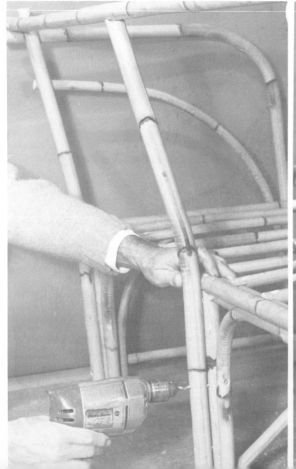
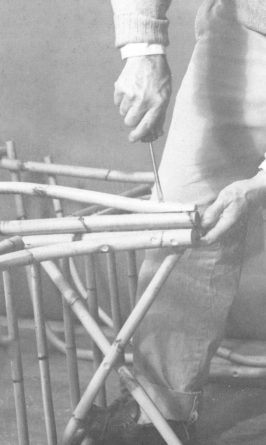

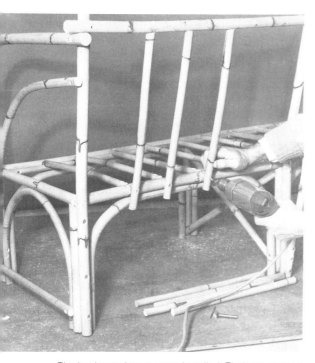
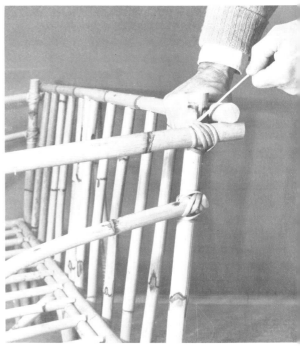

The backrest slats are now installed. Their top ends go beneath the backrest top bar, while their bottom ends are fastened to the basic seat frame.

The joints at the top ends and sides of the backrest are wrapped. Just a few crisscross turns do it.

Installing the backrest slats

Ten slats are used. Each is made from ¾-inch pole and is 16½ inches long. They are spaced equidistant from each other and the ends of the backrest. The top ends of the slats are chamfered to fit beneath the backrest top bar. The lower ends of the slats rest against back of the seat frame. The same wood screws are used on both ends of the slats; 1¼-inch #8's top and bottom. The tops of the slats are held by screws driven down through the top bar. The bottoms of the slats are held in place by screws driven sideways through the poles and into the seat frame.

FINISHING UP

Wrap the joints at the top ends and sides of the backrest with binding cane. Just a few crisscross turns will do it. You can also wrap other joints if you wish, but there is really no need for it.

Now check the front end of the seat frame to make certain the side poles do not project too far beyond the frame. If so, cut or file the projections back.

Next go over all the rough cuts and surfaces with sandpaper. Give the raw edges and the surfaces of the bent portions of the poles that have lost silicon a coat or two of clear enamel or a similar finish. Last, but not least, fill all the holes with colored putty.

17
DINING ROOM CHAIRS

<table>
<tr><td>PARTS LIST</td><td>Back legs</td><td>2 pieces 1¼-inch rattan pole, 42 inches long</td></tr>
<tr><td></td><td>Front legs</td><td>2 pieces 1 + -inch rattan pole, 19 inches long</td></tr>
<tr><td></td><td>Seat frame</td><td>2 pieces 1-inch rattan pole, 16 inches long</td></tr>
<tr><td></td><td></td><td>4 pieces 1-inch rattan pole, 19 inches long</td></tr>
<tr><td></td><td>Rungs</td><td>2 pieces 1-inch rattan pole, 18 inches long</td></tr>
<tr><td></td><td></td><td>4 pieces 1-inch rattan pole, 19 inches long</td></tr>
<tr><td></td><td>Crisscross braces</td><td>2 pieces 1-inch rattan pole, 25½ inches long</td></tr>
<tr><td></td><td></td><td>2 pieces 1-inch rattan pole, 21 inches long</td></tr>
<tr><td></td><td>Arms</td><td>2 pieces 1 + -inch rattan pole, 50 inches-long</td></tr>
<tr><td></td><td>Arch braces
(straight-back chair only)</td><td>2 pieces ¾-inch rattan pole, 36 inches long</td></tr>
<tr><td></td><td>Back leg braces
(straight-back chair only)</td><td>2 pieces ¾-inch rattan pole, 34 inches long</td></tr>
<tr><td></td><td>Splint</td><td>230 feet</td></tr>
<tr><td></td><td>Wood screws</td><td>½ box 1½-inch #8 flathead
16 1¼-inch #8 flathead
8 2-inch #8 flathead</td></tr>
</table>

The reason for the plural in the title to this chapter is that two versions of the same chair are described and illustrated. One version is a straight-back, armless chair. The second version is almost identical to the first, but it has arms.

Chair use needn't be limited to dining rooms. The same chairs can be used in a sun parlor, protected porch, or even on a flagged patio, so long as the chairs do not remain in pools of water and are brought in during the winter.

The basic chair design is 29 inches high, 22 inches wide overall. Seat dimensions are 20 by 15½ inches. Seat height is 18½ inches in front and 17 inches in the rear. Should you wish to use cushions with your chairs, drop the seat height by the thickness of the cushion—when it is sat on. If you wish to use a backrest cushion, increase the depth of the seat by a like amount.

To reduce confusion, we will call the long poles that form the chair's rear legs and back the back legs. The shorter front legs will be called the front legs. The horizontal poles over which the seat is woven will be called the seat frame. The horizontal pieces below will be called the rungs, as they usually are (they may also be called stretchers).

MAKING THE BACK LEGS

The back legs are made of two pieces of 1¼-inch rattan, 42 inches long before final cutting. This leaves 4 inches of pole extending beyond the top crossbar. If you wish, you can reduce this extension by 3½ inches, but no more unless you lower the top crossbar and back support. You can also get by with slightly thinner back legs. But don't use anything thinner than a full inch; it will be too weak.

Start by drawing in chalk on the workboard a rectangle 39 inches long and 5 inches wide. Place guiding scraps of wood along three of the rectangle sides, leaving a short side open. Measure 17 inches along one side. Draw a line across the width of the rectangle at that point. Next, draw a line from one corner of the rectangle, diagonally to where the cross line meets the side of the rectangle. From this point draw another line diagonally to the opposite corner. You now have drawn an obtuse angle. This is the necessary shape of the back legs.

Place 15 inches of one pole between the jaws of the vise. Wet the pole and confine the torch flame to the area immediately above the vise. In this way you can more or less confine the bend to this point. Check the bent pole against the drawing. Make the second pole identical to the first.

Align the two ends of the back legs by pressing them against a small board nailed to the workboard. Clamp the two back legs side by side and against a right-angle support. Now measure along the surface of the workboard a distance of 16½ inches, starting at the ends of the legs that will rest on the floor. Carry this vertically to the side of the back legs. Then carry the mark across the upper sides of the two legs. This mark or line is where you will center the ¹¹⁄₁₆-inch bit you will use to drill a ½-inch-deep hole in each leg.

If you wish, you can increase the hole-to-leg-end dimension by ½ inch or so. This will mean you will or may later need to shorten the legs, but it is insurance against making the back edge of the chair seat too low.

Use the right-angle support as a guide to help you hold the drill and bit just as vertical as you can. Don't anticipate the slight angle that is necessary at these holes. The needed angle is so slight that you will have no trouble forcing the poles to go where you want them to.

This is all we will do with the rear legs at this time. If you are making a number of chairs and have already made one and are certain of where all the holes in the back legs go, you can drill them now. But it is advisable on the first go to do no more to the legs at this time. It is slower this way, but safer.

The back legs have been bent and cut to length. Here they are clamped together to a right-angle support. Now, 11/16-inch holes ½-inch deep are being drilled into the legs. The centers of the holes are 16½ inches from the lower ends of the legs as measured on top of the workboard. In other words, when the legs are vertical, the centers of the holes will be 16½ inches above the floor. The right-angle support serves to both hold the legs upright and guide the craftsman in holding the drill perfectly vertical.

**MAKING AND ASSEMBLING THE
FRONT LEGS AND SEAT FRAME**

Each front leg is made of 1 + -inch stock and is 19 inches long leaving about ¼ inch to be trimmed at a later time. Round and smooth the top ends of the two legs. Measure down exactly 1 inch on each leg. Using this mark as the center, drill an ¹¹⁄₁₆-inch hole ½ inch deep in each pole.

Next, cut two pieces of 1-inch pole exactly 16 inches long. Reduce the diameter of both pole ends to ¹¹⁄₁₆ inch for a distance of ½ inch or a fraction more. The pole ends become the tenons, while the holes in the legs become the mortises of the joints you will make.

The easy way to do this is to drill an ¹¹⁄₁₆-inch hole in a piece of 1-inch scrap and keep this on your workbench. Then use this to test the end of the rattan as you cut its diameter down. If you have a power grindstone, remove the last inch of silicon from the pole ends. With a razor knife cut away at the pole end. When you are fairly close to the desired diameter, use the grindstone to finish the job. If you have no grindstone, just use the razor knife. The end of the pole does not have to be perfectly round where it enters the hole. It just should fit snugly.

When you have prepared all four ends of the two, 16-inch-long poles, place the end of one pole in one of the holes you have cut in one front leg. Lay the leg on the workboard, the pole that will form the side of the seat frame flat on the workboard. Now, with the aid of a square, drill an ¹¹⁄₁₆-inch hole into the same leg end. Make this hole vertical to the workboard and its center 2 inches down from the "top" end of the front leg.

The hole, or mortise, that will carry the seat's front bar is being drilled into one front leg. In order to make certain the hole being drilled will be at the necessary right angle to the side of the chair, the bar forming the side of the seat has been temporarily positioned in its hole.

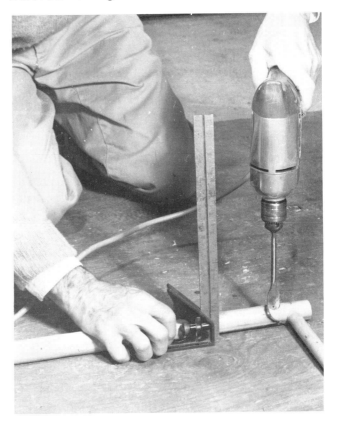

This done, make a second ½-inch-deep hole in the same leg exactly parallel to the first hole. Make the center of the second hole 11 inches down from the center of the first hole.

Repeat this on the second front leg. At this point you will have two holes 11 inches apart, facing the same direction on one leg, with a third hole facing in a direction at right angles to the other holes.

Next, cut two poles exactly 19 inches long from 1-inch stock. Taper their ends to fit the $^{11}/_{16}$-inch mortise holes we have made so far, and which we will make for all the other mortise-and-tenon joints. Join the two front legs by means of the two 19-inch poles. We now have a rectangular frame forming the front of the chair.

Check the frame to make certain it is square. If it is not, try exchanging the poles; try turning one or both poles in their holes. If necessary, remove and bend one or both poles a little.

The front two legs have been joined by the seat frame's front bar and the front rung. The combination square is used to make certain the joints are square.

When the front portion of the chair is satisfactorily square, drill through the legs and into the pole ends — seat frame and rung respectively — as necessary to install 1¼-inch #8 screws. Make the screws snug, but do not make them tight. Do not add glue to the joints either at this time.

Place the frame we have just assembled flat on the workboard. We have on hand, at this point, two 16-inch poles — the sides of the seat frame. A mortise hole must now be drilled into each pole. The hole is like all the previous holes. It is ½ inch deep and drilled with an $^{11}/_{16}$-inch bit. Center these holes 1½ inches from the ends of the poles that will fit into the rear legs.

Insert these poles — the sides of the seat frames — into the open holes near the tops of the front legs.

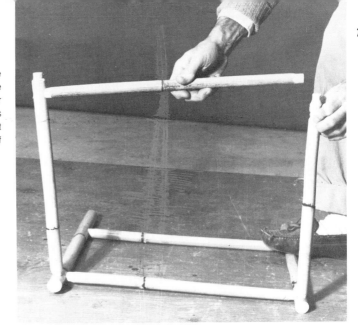

Assembly is continued. The front legs are lying on the workboard. The sides of the seat frame have been inserted in their holes. Now the seat frame's rear bar is being inserted into its holes. Note that these holes are 1 ½ inches from the end of the seat frame's side bars.

Next, cut another piece of 1-inch rattan exactly 19 inches long. Taper its ends to the desired diameter. Insert this pole, which forms a part of the rear of the seat frame, into the open holes in the sides of the seat frame poles. Now you have assembled the front of the chair and the attached seat frame.

MAKING AND ASSEMBLING A PORTION OF THE CHAIR BACK

At this point we incorporate the two back legs. Each leg has one mortise positioned near the center of the bend in the leg. Each mortise accepts the tenon (taper) on the end of each seat frame side pole. So the next step consists of pressing the rear legs into position on the seat frame sides.

This done, adjust the rear legs until they are parallel or as parallel as you can make them. Measure from the center of one leg to the center of the other. This distance should be exactly 19 inches. If so, cut three 1-inch poles to this length and taper their ends as before. (If not, vary the figure to suit your chair.) Following that, measure up from the bottoms of the rear legs 5½ inches and drill two facing mortise holes. Now measure up another 18 inches and drill two more facing holes. Finally, measure up another 13 inches and drill another pair of facing holes.

The rear legs have been positioned over the ends of seat frame side bars, and the rung joining the lower end of the rear legs has also been put in place. Before you proceed, you should check the distances between the bottom ends of the rear legs and their top ends to make sure the legs are parallel.

The three 19-inch poles you just cut and tapered fit into these facing holes. Then drill through the rear legs as necessary to insert screws that will hold these three poles in place and screws that will hold the legs to the sides of the seat frame. Use 1¼-inch #8 screws for all the joints except those between the rear legs and the seat frame. Use 1½-inch screws there. (The accompanying illustrations show that I installed the bottom pole and left the upper pieces until later, which you can also do, if you prefer.)

COMPLETING THE CHAIR FRAME

Stand the chair on its legs. Examine all the joints; see that those that should be square are square. Check the pitch on the chair seat frame. Shorten the legs if and where necessary.

Installing the side rungs

Measure 3½ inches up from the bottoms of all four legs. Drill two pairs of facing mortise holes in the four legs. Cut two pieces of 1-inch rattan 18½ inches long. (It's wise to measure the distance between the facing mortise holes — from within the holes themselves — to double-check that the distance doesn't vary somewhat in your case.) Taper the four ends as before. Insert these two pieces, which become side rungs, in the facing holes in the front and rear legs. Drill through the legs and countersink for 1½-inch #8 screws. Install the screws, but do not make them more than snug.

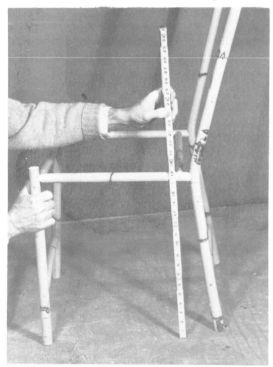

The chair has been placed in its normal upright position. The side of the seat frame where it is being measured should be 17 inches above the floor. The front top surface of the same piece of rattan should be 18½ inches above the floor. If these dimensions differ from what you want, now is the time to disassemble the chair and shorten the legs.

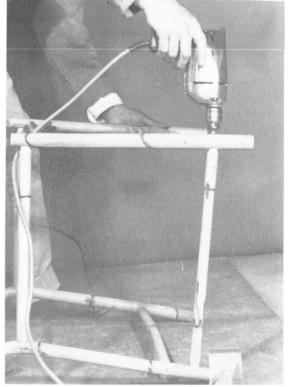

When all the measurements are correct, drill and countersink the joints and fasten them with screws.

Completing the seat frame   Cut a piece of 1-inch pole exactly 19 inches long. Chamfer both ends very carefully. This pole slips down between the top ends of the front legs. The fit must be good because you are later going to put some side pressure on this pole.

Drill upward through the front bar that is positioned beneath the chamfered bar you just positioned. Make three holes for 1¼-inch #8 screws. Drive three screws partly through the holes. Later you will tighten them.

At this point you have two lengths of 1-inch rattan reaching across the front legs. The purpose of this arrangement is to bring the front surface of the seat frame on a level with its other three sides, and yet not to cut mortise holes in the front legs that will be very close to the other mortise holes.

Now go to the rear of the seat frame. Cut another piece of 1-inch stock 19 inches long. Chamfer both ends of the pole and slip the pole behind the pole now forming the rear side of the seat frame. This done, you have two pieces of rattan side by side here. (In the front you have two pieces of rattan one above the other.) Next drill two or three holes through the pole you have just positioned and into the adjoining piece of rattan. Drive screws through the holes, but do not tighten them.

The front of the seat frame is made of two pieces of 1inch rattan. The lower piece is mortised into the front legs. The upper piece has chamfered ends and slips down between the front legs. Here, holes are being drilled up through the lower bar comprising the front of the seat frame. Later, screws will be driven through these holes to hold the upper bar in place.

The rear of the seat frame is also made of two bars. The inner bar is mortised to the side bars, the rearmost bar is not. Its ends are chamfered and it slips into place between the two side bars. Screws are used to hold it in place.

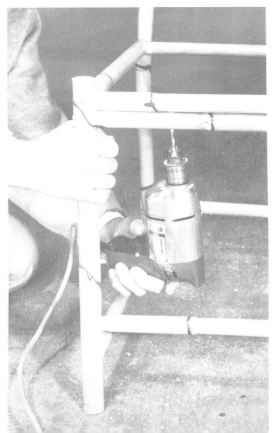

Bracing the seat frame

Two pairs of crisscross braces made of 1-inch rattan are used. One pair of braces go diagonally across near the bottom of the chair from leg to leg. The ends of these two braces are chamfered and held in place by 1½-inch #8 screws. Each brace is 25½ inches long and is positioned so that its ends rest against either the front and rear or side rungs. Where the braces cross each other, they are joined by a 1½-inch #8 screw. If the chair legs are not quite orthagonal, this is a good chance to push or pull them into position by making the braces a little shorter or longer than the available space.

The second pair of crisscross braces join just the rear legs. Each brace is 21 inches long; again cut from 1-inch stock. These braces are mortised, so the ends of the rattan have to be tapered to $^{11}/_{16}$ inch — the size of the drill used.

The lower holes for the braces are positioned 7 inches above the lower ends of the legs. The top holes are positioned 15½ inches above the lower ends of the legs. These distances are not critical, but if you make the holes farther apart, you will need slightly longer braces.

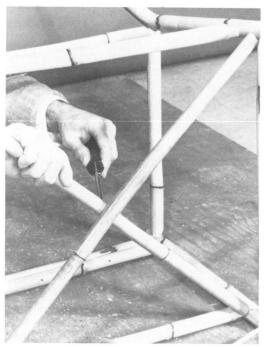

Completing the crisscross brace. A screw is being used to join the two poles where they cross. Note that the ends of these braces are chamfered. They are not mortised into the legs.

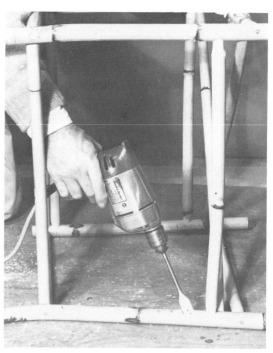

One of the holes that will accept the crisscross braces that help stiffen the back side of the chair is being drilled. Make these holes shallow. You just need sufficient depth to keep the brace end from slipping.

Anyway, make the mortise holes shallow; just deep enough to hold the pole ends or tenons in place. One brace can be reasonably straight, but you will have to force or bend the other a little to get it over the first. Again, join the two braces at the crossover point with a 1½-inch screw. Fasten the braces to the legs with screws of similar size.

Your chair frame is now complete. From here on you can make it a straight-back chair (see the instructions below for installing the arch braces) or an arm chair, as you wish, but nothing more, except weaving the seat and back, need to be done to the frame. One more exception: If you wish, you can now take the entire chair apart — taking care to identify each joint so that you can reassemble without any problems — and cover each tenon with a dab of glue and then reassemble the chair. Without the glue to hold the joints tight the chair will squeak a little when you sit on it. Otherwise it is plenty strong and will not fall apart. Also, you can tighten the frame screws at this time.

If you are going to make it a straight-back chair, you may want to cut and bend the arch braces now. But these can be left until later — no matter.

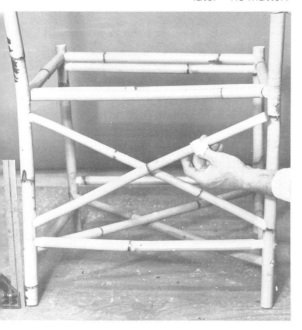

Slip the second crisscross brace into place. The chair has to be partially disassembled to do this.

If you are making a straight-back chair, this is a good time to make the arch brace needed on each side of the chair (This can even be done before the rear-leg cross braces have been installed, as in this photograph.) Here, the curve on the partially completed brace is checked against the space into which it is to be fitted.

WEAVING THE SEAT AND BACK   Reed splint is used for both the seat and back. About 230 lineal feet — including waste — will be needed. The task is easy enough, it just will take time. The only tool that you will need that hasn't been listed is a stapler. Any kind will do but the staple must have legs that are at least long enough to go through two layers of splint and still curl over a bit. Staples with ⁵⁄₁₆-inch legs are about right. Quarter-inch staples are the very smallest that will do.

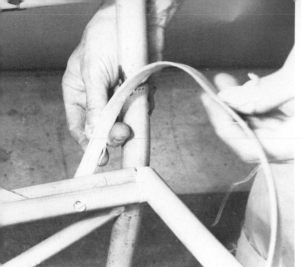
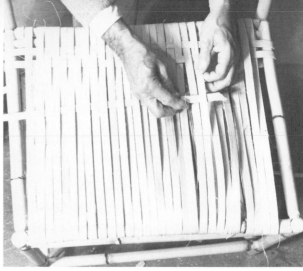

Fasten the starting end of the seat splint in place. The screws holding the two rear seat-frame poles together have been loosened. The splint is slipped between the bars. When the screws are tightened, the splint is locked in place.

Weave the chair's seat. Note that the splint goes over and under the seat frame's top front bar. After the weaving has been completed, screws are driven through the lower bar and into the upper bar.

Start by soaking the splint in water for an hour or so. Slip one end of the splint between the two poles forming the rear of the seat frame. Tighten the near screw to lock the splint in place. Now bring the splint forward and over the top of the upper front pole of the seat frame and then under it. From there the splint goes back over the end of the seat and continues around and around until the entire seat area is covered.

Incidentally, splint has one side that is smoother than the other. Try to keep this side up.

Leave a little space between the strands, say 1/16 inch or so. Do not pull the splint tight, but do not permit it to sag either. Splint ends are joined by overlapping one piece with the other by four inches or so. Then four staples are driven through both pieces of splint. Should the end of one splint come out on top of the seat, you have no choice but to cut it back so that the splice is made under the seat where it will be invisible. This is what makes for a heck of a lot of waste (about 15 percent, which is figured in the given footage).

This takes care of the splint that runs front to back. Now the splint has to be cross-woven. Start by locking the end of the splint between either the front or rear pair of seat frame bars. Push the end of the splint crosswise between the in-place strands. Direct the cross-running splint end so that it goes up and over one front-to-back strand and then under the next and so on. Upon reaching the side of the seat frame, the splint goes over the frame and is woven between the under-seat strands there just the same way. As before, if a splint ends above the seat, that splint end has to be cut back so that the splice can be made out of sight.

Technically there is nothing difficult about weaving the splint. The one-over-one-under pattern is easy enough. The only problem is that one tends to fall asleep and then you have to backtrack and start over again.

Keep the splint soft and pliable by wetting it down as you go. Cut a point on its end to facilitate slipping it through. Lock the end between either of the two parallel end bars. If you have difficulty passing the splint through the in-place strands, try using a screwdriver and a pair of longnose pliers to push and pull the splint through. Note that the side-to-side strands cannot be positioned close together. At best they will be about 1 inch apart. To make these strands closer to one another, the strands running the other way have to be spaced farther apart.

The back of the chair is woven the same way. Start by drilling and countersinking a ¼-inch hole through one of the back rungs 3 inches in from the side of the rear leg. Fold the end of the water-soaked splint and force it through the hole. When you bend the splint around and start weaving, the splint will be locked in place.

Wrap the vertical strands around the upper and lower rungs of the chair's back leaving about ¹⁄₁₆ of an inch between the strands. Fasten the end of the splint to one rung by drilling and countersinking another ¼-inch hole in the rung. Then fold the splint and pull it through the hole.

The horizontal strand of splint is also started in a hole. This time the hole is through one rear leg, positioned 3 inches down from the top rung. The cross weave is also terminated in a hole, this one 3 inches above the center rung on the chair back.

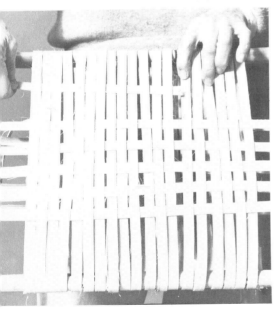

Weave the back of the seat. The splint that runs vertically is woven first. The splint that runs horizontally is woven next.

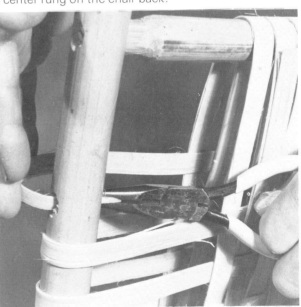

Here is how the splint on the back of the chair is begun and terminated. When you fold the splint's end and pull it through the hole, you must also push it from the other side.

MAKING AND ATTACHING THE ARMS

Each arm is made from a 50-inch-long piece of 1+-inch rattan. It is fastened by screws to the back leg and the side of the seat frame. This sets up a diagonal brace that stiffens the entire assembly far more than might be imagined from its appearance.

You can bend each arm by placing 12 inches of the pole in your vise and heating a 6-inch-or-so area to produce a medium radius bend, and then judge the results by placing the bent pole against the side of the chair. Or, you can draw a rectangle on the workboard with chalk, draw the angle and curve within it, and then work to that. The rectangle necessary is 18 inches wide, 24 inches long. The curve is drawn in one corner and then angles back to the diagonal corner. In other words you need a V shape with unequal sides.

When you have secured the arm you desire and know it is correct by temporarily fastening it to the side of the chair, bend the second arm to match the first. Then you can fasten both of them.

The top of the arm is fastened with a 2-inch #8 screw to the rear leg at a point about 26 inches above the floor. The bottom of the arm is fastened with a similar screw 4 inches above the floor. The curved portion of the arm is fastened to the side of the seat frame about 6 inches back from the front surface of the front leg. None of these dimensions are critical. The arm rest will look best if its top surface is parallel with the top of the seat.

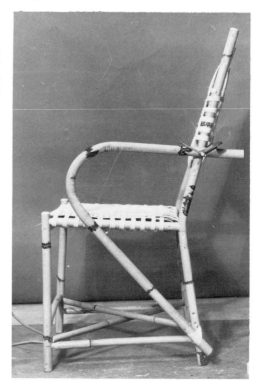

An arm is fastened in position with a clamp and some masking tape. Note that the arm is roughly parallel to the seat. Now the center and lower screw holes can be drilled and countersunk. With two screws in, the clamp can be removed and the necessary screw driven home in that position.

MAKING THE STRAIGHT-BACK CHAIR

No arms are used. Instead the sides of the chair are braced with arch braces and the back legs of the chair are braced with a slightly bent or curved length of ¾-inch rattan.

Making and installing the arch braces

Each brace is made from a 36-inch-long piece of ¾-inch rattan. Each brace is curved to fit a space 16 inches wide and 13 inches high. Since there is a straight brace holding the legs in fixed

An arch brace has been fastened in place on the straight-back chair. Now the back leg brace is fastened in place with screws. Note how the ends of the brace have been slightly bent and tapered.

relationship, you do not need to be accurate with the arch braces. You can snap them into place or pull them apart a little when you fasten them to the bottom of the seat sides and legs. Use 5 1¼-inch #8 screws for each brace.

Making and installing the back leg braces

Each back leg brace is made from a 34-inch-long piece of rattan. The last 4 inches of each brace is bent at a slight angle. Then the ends of the braces are tapered along one side so that the brace can rest fairly smoothly against the rear sides of the rear chair legs. Six 1¼-inch #8 screws are used to fasten each brace in place. When this is done, there is a space of about 3 or 4 inches between the center of the brace and the center of the rear leg.

FINISHING UP

As with any other piece of rattan furniture, finishing consists of removing all the rough edges, sealing all the raw edges and the places where the silicon has fallen from the sides of the poles, and also filling all the holes with colored putty.

With the chair, however, there is an additional task. The woven splint should be sealed with any clear lacquer, enamel, or varnish. If this is not done, the highly porous splint will be quickly soiled. After the sealer has dried, cut the whiskers and fuzz off with a razor knife and a touch of fine sandpaper.

18
NIGHT TABLE

PARTS LIST		
	Top	1 piece ¾-inch chipboard, 14 by 14 inches
		1 piece tight cane webbing, 14 by 14 inches
		2 pieces 1-inch rattan pole, 16 inches long, split in half
		2 pieces 1-inch rattan pole, 14 inches long, split in half
		1 piece ⅜-inch rattan pole, 72 inches long
	Shelf	1 piece ¾-inch chipboard, 9½ by 8¾ inches
		2 pieces 1-inch rattan pole, 11 inches long
		2 pieces 1-inch rattan poles, split in half, 9½ inches long
		1 piece tight cane webbing, 10 by 10 inches
		1 piece ⅜-inch rattan pole, 48 inches long
	Legs	4 pieces, 1-inch rattan pole, 32 inches long
	Arch braces	2 pieces 1-inch rattan pole, 22 inches long
	Wood screws	4 1½-inch #8 flathead
		10 1¼-inch #8 flathead
	Nails	40 ¾ inch #18 brads
		26 4-penny finishing

While it may be a moot question as to whether the table pictured should be classified as a night table, utility table, telephone stand, flower stand, lamp stand, favorite uncle's urn support, or checkers table, there is no question but that it is attractive and useful.

As it stands, the table is 27½ inches high, the top is 15½ inches square, and the duck feet spread an overall distance of 21 inches. The shelf is 9½ by 11 inches overall and 11 inches up from the floor.

The height and other dimensions chosen make this table useful for all the purposes mentioned and possibly some others that do not come to mind at this time.

DESIGN VARIATIONS

The major design change that you may want to consider is the elimination of the "feet" on the bottom of the legs. It will stand almost as well without them, and the bends do require additional material and labor. However, the curves or bends do add a lot more charm.

You might also consider replacing the cane webbing with burlap. This would introduce no problems. The same technique described in the making of an étagère would be used to apply the burlap to the table parts.

The ⅜-inch rattan trim, or border, on the shelf and top should not be eliminated unless you have a specific reason for wanting a perfectly flat surface. The borders give the table a finished look and contribute a great deal to its beauty.

Dimensions can be varied within reason. If you do change any one of them, try to hold the overall appearance of the table proportional to the original design.

MAKING THE LEGS

Each leg is 32 inches long before bending and is cut from poles a full inch thick or thicker. The single right angle bend of the end of the leg is made as tight — small radius — as possible.

Start by drawing in chalk on the workboard a rectangle 27½ inches long and 6 inches wide. Place one guide board along one long side of the rectangle, and a second guide board along a short side.

Place the leg inside the vise so that the pole is in a vertical position between the jaws of the vise and 2½ inches of the pole is below the top edges of the vise jaws and clamped between them.

Confine the torch flame to the area immediately above the jaws of the vise and try for a perfect or near perfect right angle at this point. Remove the bent leg and check it against your guide. Correct the bend if necessary and then cut one or both ends of the leg so that when the leg is pressed against the aforementioned guides, neither the short nor long portion of the leg extends beyond the chalk rectangle. Do this to the other three poles to make a total of four legs.

Place one leg in the vise with the bend up. With a file or a Surform plane, remove a sufficient amount from the bottom side of the pole to make a flat surface ½ inch wide or more at the very end of the leg. When the table is standing, the table leg will rest on this

Check the bend on a leg against the guide. When the angle at the left is made a bit sharper, the leg end will align with the chalk mark.

flat surface. Do this to all four legs. Do not worry about making the flat surfaces on each leg bottom identical. It is not necessary.

MAKING THE TABLETOP   The top of the table is cut from ¾-inch-thick chipboard. The top is a square 14 by 14 inches in size.

Place the tabletop on the workboard and draw two diagonal lines across the chipboard, from corner to corner. Measure inward along each line for a distance of 2½ inches, and mark the spot with a pencil. Now, carefully drill an $^{11}/_{16}$-inch hole through the chipboard at each mark you have made, for a total of four holes. When you drill, take care to keep the drill bit vertical to the surface of the chipboard. This is all we do to the tabletop at this time.

ASSEMBLY   The bottom ends of the poles, as stated, comprise the bent ends. The top ends of the legs are straight, or nearly so. Reduce the diameter of the last ¾ inch of the top of each leg to a fraction more than $^{11}/_{16}$ of an inch. If you have a power grinder, remove the silicon from the leg ends for a distance of an inch or a little more. Then cut the leg end down to the required diameter with a razor knife. It is easy enough if you take off a sliver at a time and rotate the rattan after each cut. The reason for using the grindstone is that the silicon tends to dull the razor knife; but you can cut through the silicon and rattan almost as easily as you can cut through the wood alone.

When you have prepared the four leg ends, poke each end through a hole in the tabletop. Stand the table upright. Make the legs as vertical as you can. Space them evenly apart. Now measure down to the floor or workboard from the tabletop at each of its corners to the floor. You want 26½ inches or so, now in order to end up with 27 inches to the surface of the finished top. (The trim, of course projects a fraction higher.) In any case, you want the same figure at all four corners, so remove what is necessary from the high leg either from the bottom of the leg—the flat area—or from the shoulder of the mortise joint that supports the tabletop. When the table top is level to within ¼-inch or less, you can go on to the next step.

Lock the bottoms of the legs in relation to each other by surrounding them with scraps of wood, or cleats, nailed to the workboard. Position the cleats so that the bends are in line with one another and parallel, and so that the ends of the legs are also in line. Space the lower ends of the legs apart the same distances as their tops are. In other words, the legs are held in the exact same position you want them to be when the table is completed.

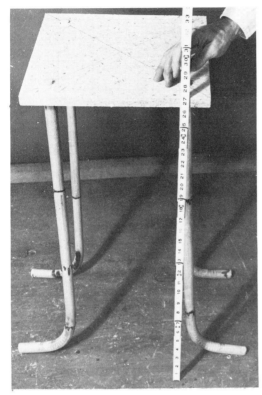

The legs have been temporarily positioned in the holes in the tabletop. Now a rough check of the height of the table at all four corners is made.

Scraps of wood, or cleats, are lightly nailed to the workboard around the leg "feet." The guides hold the legs immobile while you work on them.

MAKING AND INSTALLING THE SHELF

Measure 11 inches up from the workboard along each leg and mark the spot with a pencil. These four marks locate the center of the four $1\frac{1}{16}$-inch holes you will drill in each leg. Each hole is $\frac{1}{2}$ inch deep and is cut parallel to the table's feet and parallel to the workboard. The holes are the mortises for the mortise-and-tenon joints that hold in place the bars forming the sides of the shelf. Each hole faces an identical hole on the other leg of the same side of the table.

This done, measure from the center of one leg to the center of the second leg. The dimension should be equal or slightly larger than the distance from the bottom of one hole to the bottom of the facing hole. In our case the dimension is $10\frac{1}{2}$ inches. In your case it may be a little different, even if you are making an identical table, because of varying rattan thickness and bends in the poles. You may also find the length of the second pole that supports the other side of the shelf may be slightly different from our length and your first measurement. In any case, cut two pieces of 1-inch rattan to whatever lengths are necessary. Then taper their ends to fit into the mortise holes you have cut.

Installing the shelf-support bars

You will have to remove one of each pair of the table's legs from its restrictions to do this. Once the bars are installed, check the spread of the legs to see that they are still correct — legs parallel. If not, increase the depth of the holes, shorten the tenons on the pole ends, or stuff some sawdust and glue into the holes to reduce their depth, depending on the correction required.

When the bar lengths are correct, drill through the legs and into the ends of the tenons. Countersink the holes and fasten the legs with 1½-inch #8 screws.

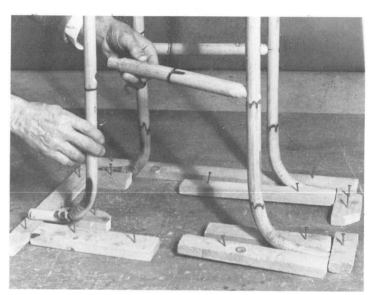

Facing mortise holes have been drilled into the legs. Now the shelf-support bars are installed.

Cutting and fastening the shelf

The shelf fits between the two shelf-support bars — the horizontal pieces of rattan joining the legs. Since these pieces may not be straight, and since they are somewhat tapered, you have to measure their separation and cut the shelf to fit. In our case, the shelf width is exactly 9½ inches. So that the ¾-inch chipboard would not have to be cut, the facing surfaces of the supporting bars were cut back a little with a Surform plane.

The length of the shelf is about 1 inch less than the length of the supporting bars. In this case the length worked out to be 8¾ inches. So, the shelf we used was 9½ by 8¾ inches in size.

The shelf is now placed between its supporting bars and positioned so that the bottom surface of the chipboard is flush with the lower surfaces of the supporting bars, and the ends of the shelf are spaced equidistant from the table legs. Four holes are drilled and countersunk through the two supporting bars and into the chipboard — two holes through each bar. Next, four 1¼-inch #8 screws are driven through the holes into the shelf.

The distance between the supporting bars is measured. This will be the width of the shelf. If necessary, the facing surfaces of the supporting bars will be cut back a little with a file or Surform plane.

The shelf has been cut and positioned. Now screws are being driven through the supporting bars and into the edge of the shelf. The lower surface of the shelf has been made flush with the lower surface of the supporting bars.

MAKING AND FASTENING THE ARCH BRACES

Two braces are used. They join the legs to the underside of the tabletop. Each brace is made from a 22-inch-long piece of ¾-inch rattan. Since the two legs are locked top and bottom — by the table top and the shelf, the braces do not have to be perfect. You can press them in or pull them into position. Use the table itself as a guide when you bend the braces. Fasten them in place with three 1¼-inch #8 screws each.

The arch braces are installed. If the top screw goes through the tabletop, file its point flush with the chipboard.

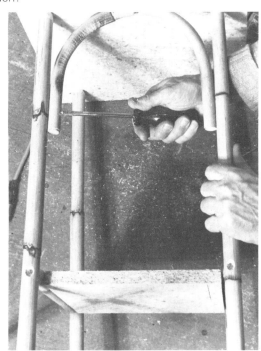

COMPLETING THE SIDES OF THE SHELF

We stopped work on the shelf to make and install the arch braces. They could be installed later. But this was the sequence followed in building this table, so this is the way the work is described.

At this point we have a shelf with rattan along two sides. Two sides of the shelf are exposed. These sides are now covered with split rattan. In our case we start with a piece of 1-inch stock 9½ inches long. It is split in half. Each half is nailed to opposite sides of the chipboard using 4-penny finishing nails. The lower edges of the split rattan are made flush with the bottom of the shelf. Three nails a side are plenty. If you drill pilot holes using a $\frac{1}{16}$-inch bit through the rattan, you will find you will not bend any of the nails and the nailing will be lots easier.

The exposed shelf edge is covered with split rattan nailed in place. Drilling pilot holes through the split rattan will save you a lot of fuss and bent nails.

APPLYING THE CANE WEBBING

Remove the tabletop from its legs. Apply a little glue to each leg. Replace the legs in the tabletop. Drive the top firmly down on the legs. Let it stand until the glue has dried. Then, use a hacksaw and cut the tops of the legs flush with the tabletop. Follow up with sandpaper or a Surform plane and make certain none of the legs project at all above the tabletop.

If the tops of the legs protrude through the top of the table, cut the protrusions flush with the chipboard. Note the diagonal pencil lines that served to locate the holes in the chipboard.

You will need closely woven cane webbing. The top requires a piece that is 14 by 14 inches. The shelf needs a piece the size of the chipboard, which in our case is 9½ by 8½ inches. Soak the cane until it is soft. Spread a generous layer of glue — Elmer's is fine — over the chipboard, taking care to make the layer even and complete, especially along the edges. Press the webbing atop the glue. Make the webbing flat and hold it in place with weights or boards and clamps. Now wait until the glue has dried and the webbing is also dry and firmly in place.

Now with the razor knife cut the webbing flush with the edges of the chipboard. The easy way to do this is to upend the table on the workboard and run the knife's point along the cane again and again until it separates. The piece of webbing that goes on the shelf should, of course, have been cut to fit before being positioned.

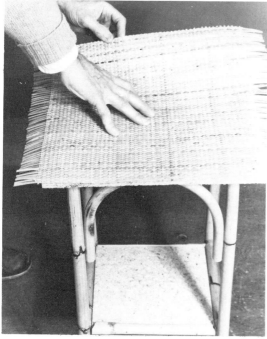 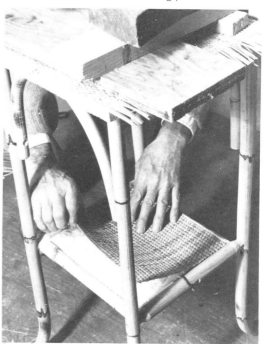

The top of the table is covered with a layer of glue, then the well-soaked webbing is pressed firmly on top. Boards and weights are used to hold the webbing down until it and the glue dry.

A piece of webbing is cut to fit the shelf. The webbing is soaked for a few hours. The top of the shelf is then covered with glue and the webbing is pressed firmly down against it. Weights and/or clamps and boards are used to hold the webbing flat and in place until the glue dries.

COMPLETING THE TOP AND SHELF

The cane webbing has been securely glued in place. The edges of the cane are flush with the edges of the chipboard. Now we have to hide the chipboard with split rattan. You need one piece of 1-inch rattan 16 inches long and one piece 14 inches long. Split both pieces down their middles. Drill four or five ⅟₁₆-inch pilot holes through each piece of split rattan. Fasten two pieces of split rattan to the tabletop. The ends of these two long pieces overlap the ends of the table. Use 4-penny finishing nails. Then fasten one short piece of split rattan to one of the remaining two sides of the table. Make its bottom edge flush with the bottom of the chipboard. Make its ends flush with the ends of the board. Use 4-penny finishing nails to do the job. Fasten the second short piece of split rattan similarly in place to the opposite side of the tabletop. Now, with a file or sandpaper or Surform plane round the ends of the long pieces of split rattan to conform to the adjoining surfaces.

Pieces of split rattan are nailed along the sides of the tabletop. The two pieces shown in place project beyond the edges of the table. The two pieces to be nailed on will fit between the first two. Then the corners of the first two pieces of split rattan will be filed down.

Fastening the ⅜-inch trim   Cut a 45-degree angle on the end of a piece of ⅜-inch rattan. Place the rattan along any edge of the tabletop with the cut end at a corner of the table. Using ¾-inch #18 brads, fasten the trim in the crack between the edge of the table and the surface of the split rattan. Use about one brad every four or so inches. When you come to the end of the side, cut the trim at an angle with the aid of

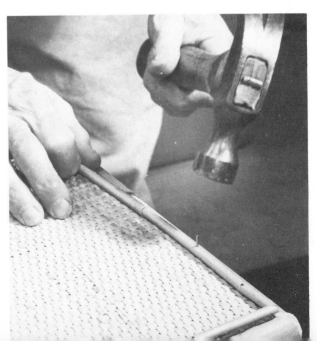

The ⅜-inch rattan trim is nailed to the top of the table and the shelf.

the razor knife. Make the cut in line with the corner and at 45 degrees to the length of the trim. In other words, line the knife up with the two diagonal corners and cut straight down. Cut the starting end of a second piece of rattan at an angle matching the end of the in-place rattan trim. Then nail the second piece of trim in place, and keep repeating this operation until you have done the four sides of the tabletop.

The shelf is trimmed the same way. All in all, you will need about 10 feet of thin rattan trim.

The completed shelf with the trim in place.

FINISHING UP   Sand all the rough and raw edges smooth. Fill all the holes with putty colored with a little ocher. Seal all the cut pole ends and all the rattan areas that have lost their layer of silicon with some sort of clear varnish or enamel.

Sealing the webbing   If you do not plan to use the table for any purpose that might lead to food or drink being spilled on it, you need not do anything to the cane webbing. However, if there is a chance of this, it is wise to give the webbing several coats of a clear sealer. The purpose is to fill the cracks between the strands of cane so that soil cannot get in between. Since you will need a lot of sealer, it is best to apply it with a brush. There is too little liquid in a spray can; half of it is air and a fraction always remains in the bottom of the can.

That does it.

Part Three
Repairs

19
REPAIRING RATTAN AND WICKER PIECES

DAMAGED PAINT ON RATTAN
Spot painting

It is no trick at all to apply a little paint to the bare spots on a piece of rattan furniture. It is, however, a minor chore to make the spot paint job blend smoothly with the old paint and a major trick, sometimes, to match the color of the new paint to the old.

Making it all smooth

Start by sandpapering the area to be painted and the edges of the adjoining, old paint with #200 (very fine) sandpaper. This is done to remove all oils and finger marks that may be on the surface to be painted, and to remove the sharp edge that exists between the paint and the bare wood. The area that has been sanded is wiped clean with a dry piece of cloth. Then the new paint is applied with a spray can. Care is taken to apply the paint evenly and to cover a portion of the old paint surrounding the bare spot as well as the spot itself.

The first coat is permitted to dry hard and then lightly sanded with the same grade of fine sandpaper. The dust is removed with a clean cloth and a second coat of paint is sprayed on. This coat is also permitted to dry hard, sanded, and sprayed a third time.

The following step depends on the paint you have used. If you have applied an enamel, it will dry with a shine. So, if it is shine you want and the new paint is level with the surface of the old and there is no visible edge between the new and the old paint, you need do no more.

If there is a visible edge, and we are speaking of paint surface ridges, not color, you need to keep sanding and painting until the ridges are gone.

If you have used a quick-drying lacquer, which does not dry with a shine, and you want a shine, let the paint dry really hard. Then go over it with #400 sandpaper. (Both these grades of paper can be purchased in an auto supply shop.)

Matching paint colors

This is often a major trick and sometimes an impossible trick. The color of paint varies in several ways. Depending on the color, the paint may fade. And, no matter what the original color may be, with time the paint will go toward both white and black. So that a bright green will eventually turn into a pale, whitish, dirty green.

If you have the eye of a Vermeer, you can mix the necessary colors and match the balance of the aged paint. But if you are only an ordinary mortal and have to select from the colors available in spray cans, the chance of a match is not too good.

Repainting it all

For a nearly perfect job on old painted rattan, this is probably the only way to go, though of course it involves a lot more work and material.

Start as before by sanding and painting the bare spots. Keep sanding and paint the same areas until they they are perfectly smooth. Then go over the entire piece of furniture with a clean rag dipped in nonleaded gasoline to remove all traces of oil left by hands and wandering cooking aromas.

Now you can paint the furniture by standard techniques, the best of which is spraying. If you are going to paint several pieces of furniture, you might consider renting a spray gun and associate equipment. Cans work fine, but they contain very little paint.

Removing all the paint

This is called stripping, and it can be done by one of two ways. The first consists of applying a paint remover, letting it sit in place, and then wiping and scraping the resulting gook off. Following that, the entire piece is wiped down with alcohol to remove all traces of the remover. If you do not remove the remover, the paint you apply may not adhere evenly.

The second method consists of bringing the piece of furniture to a professional stripper. He will literally hose the paint off and do a far better job than you can possibly do in any reasonable length of time. The cost is not as high as you might imagine, since you will need lots of paint remover if you do the stripping yourself.

All this brings us to the reason for stripping. If you want the best possible paint job, stripping is the way to go. If you want to return the rattan to its original pristine condition, second thoughts are in order. Most often, rattan is painted to hide defects such as discoloration caused by rot. This is not reversible. So if you are seeking a nice, bright yellow piece of furniture, you most likely will be disappointed. To save time and money, scrape a little of the paint off here and there, especially near the bottoms of the legs. If the wood itself is discolored, there is nothing you can do to change it; even bleaching really will not help.

DAMAGED PAINT ON WICKER

Since wicker furniture is composed of a great number of thin strands of material, sanding and similar treatment to smooth small areas of the furniture are impractical. You have the choice of either painting the bare spots or simply repainting the entire piece of furniture.

Stripping wicker

For a smooth repaint job on an old piece of wicker that may have been painted several times before, the only practical technique is to strip the piece and start afresh. However, there is the strong possibility that it is the paint that holds the wicker in place and not the reverse. When you strip a heavily painted old piece of wicker furniture, you chance its disintegration.

LOOSE WICKER SEATS

One fairly standard practice of commercial wicker chair manufacture is to preweave the chair seat much like a basket is woven, but flat. Then the flat seat is tied to the chair by means of strands of reed. In time these strands break and the seat itself becomes loose.

Typical commercially manufactured wicker chair. The prewoven bottom or seat has come loose.

Refastening the wicker seat

The broken ends of the reed that held the seat in place are snipped off close to the underside of the seat. The end of a length of soaked cane is fastened to the chair frame with a knot. Then the cane is slipped through any of the spaces in the wicker seat and wrapped around the chair frame. This is repeated as many times as necessary until the edge of the entire seat or the loose portion of the edge is fastened in place. There is no need to make the cane wrapping even, for when you finish wrapping and repaint the edge of the chair, the cane will be almost invisible.

LEFT: The projecting ends of the reed that held the seat in place are snipped off.
RIGHT: The end of a piece of water-soaked binding cane is fastened to the seat frame, passed through an opening in the woven seat, and wrapped around the seat frame. Pulling on the cane pulls the seat back in place.

BELOW LEFT: The binding process is continued all around the seat and supporting seat frame.
BELOW RIGHT: The finished repair prior to painting.

LOOSE WICKER ARMRESTS AND BACKS

Like the seats, armrests and chair backs are usually prewoven of reed and then positioned atop the chair frame and tied in place with reed. On some furniture the reed passes through holes in the chair frame. On other furniture the reed is wrapped around the chair frame and then the frame material and the fastening reed are hidden beneath a continuous wrapping of cane.

Refastening armrests and backs

The ends of the broken holding reeds are snipped off close to the underside of the wicker part that is to be refastened. Then a number of holes are drilled through the nearest portion of the chair frame. One hole every 5 or 6 inches or so is fine. Next, soaked reed is passed through the holes in the frame and then woven into the adjoining wicker. As this is done, the reed is pulled fairly taut so as to pull the wicker armrest or back into place. Since the repair reed is of the same diameter or close to the same diameter as the balance of the wicker, the repair reed will not be noticeable.

The covering of woven reed on the back of this chair has come loose. The pieces of reed holding it in place have broken.

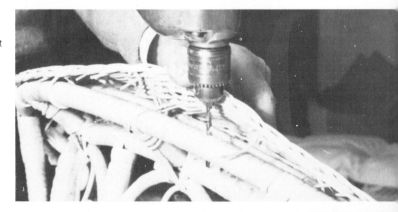

Holes are drilled about 6 inches apart through the seat frame.

Soaked reed is passed through the holes. The lower end of the reed may be nailed in place, glued in place, or just woven into the rest of the chair.

The upper end of the reed is woven into the woven reed.

LOOSE WRAPPING CANE

There are two ways to go here. One, you can completely remove the loose cane wrapping, soak a longer piece of cane in water, and wrap the area completely again. Or, you can make a quick repair.

To do the latter, unwrap a few turns of the loose cane, spread a layer of Duco or similar cement on the frame, and then replace the loose cane, making it as smooth and as tight as you can. Since the cane just fits, your only problem will be to hold it in place while the cement dries. This can be done with tape of any kind. The tape is later removed, of course.

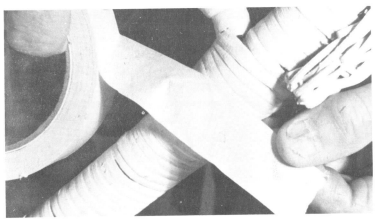

Duco or similar cement is spread under broken binding cane. Then the cane is pressed back in place and some kind of tape is used to hold it in place until the cement dries.

VERY OLD PAINTED WICKER

Very old wicker requires special care. It is fragile, but if it's repaired properly, it can be made to look reasonably well and to serve for another few years.

The prime point to bear in mind is that the less done the better. You cannot remove very much of the old wicker without it breaking up into little pieces. So whatever you remove must be replaced with new material.

Broken joints

These joints are almost invariably held together by nails and cane. In time the nails rust away and the joint separates. Remove the old nail if you can, or cut off its end. Then drill and countersink a hole through the frame and install a flathead wood screw. Next, you can rewrap the joint and whatever bare frame may exist alongside.

LEFT: A rattan furniture joint has come apart. Nail and cane that held it together have long since disintegrated. CENTER: A hole has been drilled through chair arm. Now a wood screw is driven through the same arm and into the end of the rattan pole. RIGHT: Binding cane is used to cover bare spot alongside the repaired joint. Screwdriver is holding bench members apart so that cane can be passed through.

Ornamentation

The best way to deal with broken ornamentation is to snip the broken ends off and let the furniture be. Trying to remove the supporting wrappings in order to install new ornamentation — circles, whirls, lollypops; etc. — just leads to more damage. However, on some cases where the ornamentation is actually holding parts of the wicker together, new wicker can be installed to advantage. You just have to work cautiously.

The reed weaving that originally joined the sides of this old wicker sofa have been cut off with a pair of diagonal pliers. New, soaked reed is now inserted. Since the new reed will actually help hold the old reed together, it is worthwhile installing it.

REPLACING A CANE WEBBED SEAT

This task is a lot easier than it looks. All the tools you need are a hammer, screwdriver, razor knife, and a couple of wood wedges you can easily make.

Removing the spline

The spline is the V-shape wedge that holds the cane webbing (also called machine cane) in place. This is the most difficult portion of the entire job.

Use an old screwdriver, because a new one has sharp edges, and pry the spline up and out. Do not expect to be able to use the spline again. It never happens, but you can use a piece of it as a guide to purchase a new piece of spline.

If the spline refuses to respond and you are working on a piece of furniture you plan to refinish, spread a little paint remover over the spline. Then scrape off the old varnish. Follow with some water. Let it soak in. Hopefully, the water will soften the glue and you will be able to remove the spline.

If the spline is recalcitrant, secure a narrow-blade screwdriver — or grind an old one down to the proper width and force it beneath the old spline. But take care not to damage the edges of the wood.

The spline out, use the screwdriver to clean the groove of all the old pieces of webbing. Nothing must remain and the sides of the groove must be smooth and clean. Some craftsmen use sandpaper to clean the groove. Some use a router with a bit of the proper size. In any case, if the groove is not perfectly clean, you will have difficulty installing the webbing.

Remove the spline holding the cane webbing in place on an old chair. The old webbing is torn and must be replaced Care must be exercised to remove the spline and cane without damaging the groove.

When the cane and spline have been removed, the groove must be made perfectly clean. The best tool for this is an old screwdriver, its width ground down to just fit into the groove.

Installing the webbing

Start by securing a length of spline of the correct size and long enough to fill the entire groove. In addition, you will need a piece of open webbing ½ inch larger all around than the outside edges of the groove.

Soak the webbing in water. While the webbing is soaking, make two wedges from wood. Each wedge should be about 2 inches wide and 3 inches long and cut from solid wood approximately ¼ inch thick. The end of each edge is tapered to a thickness of approximately ⅛ inch for a distance of about ¾ inch. If your chair seat has a curve in its circumference, you will also need a similarly tapered wedge about ½ inch wide.

Place the webbing shiny side up over the chair. Position the webbing evenly over the groove. Now, with the help of one wide wedge drive the webbing into the groove at the center of the rear of the seat. This is why the end of the wedge must be thin; it must be able to push the webbing all the way to the bottom of the groove. Let the wedge remain where it is. Smoothen the webbing as best you can and using the second wedge, drive the front center of the webbing into the groove. Note that the webbing should overlap the end of the wedge so that the sides of the groove are lined with webbing. If the webbing doesn't do this, the webbing is too short or you have not centered it properly. Let the second wedge remain in place.

Now go back to the first wedge. Remove it and use it to drive more webbing into the groove; first to the right of the wedge's original position, then to the left. Do a little at a time until you reach the corners. Then do the same at the front edge of the webbing. Now do the sides; again a little at a time, starting more or less at the center of each side.

Now, use the narrow wedge and do the corners. (The broad wedges will not fit around turns.) When all the sides of the webbing have been driven home, run a thick line of Elmer's or a similar glue down the entire groove. Make the line about ⅛ inch thick. You want sufficient glue to seal the webbing in place, but not so much it squirts out when you insert the spline.

Well-soaked cane webbing is placed over the chair seat. The outer edges of the new webbing extend ½ inch beyond the outer edges of the groove on all its sides. First a wedge is used to drive the central rear portion of the webbing deep into the groove. Then a second wedge is used to do the same to the central front portion of the webbing.

After the two central portions have been driven into the groove, the wedges are moved and the balance of the webbing is driven into the groove a little at a time. Round corners are done last with a narrow wedge. Following this, glue is introduced into the length of the groove.

Installing the spline   Soak the spline until it is soft. Then press it into the groove between the facing webbing surfaces. Start the spline at the back of the chair somewhere and run it around until it overlaps its own end. Then, with a razor knife, cut the spline to fit. Next, using one of the wide wedges, drive the spline into the groove as far as it will go.

Let the chair sit for a day or so until the glue has dried hard. Then, with a sharp razor knife, trim off the excess webbing that protrudes above the surface of the spline.

Next the spline is driven into the groove. It should fit snugly and lock the webbing edges in place.

When the glue has hardened, a razor knife is used to remove the projecting ends of the webbing.

REWEAVING A CHAIR   There are as many ways of weaving or reweaving a chair back or bottom as there are weavers. The following suggested method and pattern is probably one of the simplest and fastest. It may be used for new work or, as illustrated, in the replacement of an old chair bottom.

The material used is #3 ($\frac{3}{16}$ inch in diameter) sea grass. Thinner material requires more strands and thicker material is a little more difficult to work with. In place of the sea grass, which is worked dry, you can also use reed, which should be well soaked before using.

Removing the old bottom

Examine the old bottom for tips and suggestions as to how you may wish to construct the replacement seat. Check the side and rear rails for nails and splinters which may injure you while you work. You can ignore loose tops rails if you wish. Weaving a seat from sea grass will pull all the top rails together and tighten the chair.

The first step in reweaving an old seat bottom is cutting the old seat away.

Planning your pattern

All weaving, whether it be cloth or chair bottoms or backs, consists of two groups of fibers or threads called the warp and the woof. The warp is the cords or threads stretched across the frame at the start of weaving. The cross threads or strands that are woven over and under the warp strands are called the woof. In the case of chair backs and bottoms, the primary strands, the warp, is always run front to back, or vertically.

After we decide on the material we are going to use, our first step in planning our pattern consists of measuring the space available for the warp and deciding how many warp strands and their spacing are going to be used.

Available space is always limited by the smaller of the two supporting bars or rails. In this case, and usually on chairs, the back rail is the smaller. In our example, the back rail is 10½ inches long. (We shall discuss the front rail later.)

The next step is to determine just how much space a strand of our weaving material requires. In our case, we wrapped four turns of #3 sea grass around a stick and found that the space needed was 1 inch. This is because sea grass and other soft materials flatten out a bit when they are wrapped around a stick or what have you. So that is our guide: four turns, or four strand widths, to the inch.

We decided to use eight pairs of strands for the warp simply because that is what the old bottom had and simple multiplication showed it would work out evenly.

Allowing ½ inch for each pair of strands works out to 8 x ½, or 4 inches, to be occupied by the strands. Positioning a pair of strands at the ends of the rear seat rail leaves seven spaces between strand pairs. Since there is a total of 10½ inches of rail, of which 4 inches is occupied by the warp strands, there is 10½ − 4, or 6½ inches, to be divided into seven spaces between the warp strands. Each space is therefore a fraction less than an inch wide. If we squeeze, we can get four turns of #3 grass into the space of 1 inch. So that was the plan decided upon for the warp: Eight pairs of #3 grass separated by four turns between pairs.

Your chairs may work out differently, but the basic approach is the same. You may find you need more or less pairs. You may find you need more or less spacing between the pairs, or you may not wish to use pairs at all but decide to use single strands.

Front rail spacing   The front seat rail on the chair pictured is 13¼ inches long. This means it is 2¾ inches longer than the rear bar. We can correct for this by making the spacing between the warp strands greater along the front bar, or we can simply cover as much of the ends of the front bars with turns of sea grass. This is by far the simpler method, so this is what was done. The difference of 2¾ inches was divided in half and each half measured off on the ends of the front bar, and the point marked in pencil. The plan calls for the warp strands to line up with these marks. In this way we are able to keep the warp strands running at a right angle to the front and back of the chair.

Installing the warp strands   The sea grass is cut into a number of pieces, each three times the distance from the front to the rear rail. Each piece of sea grass is then folded exactly in half.

Two inches of the folded grass is held firmly against the inside of the front rail. Then the balance of the pair of strands is wrapped tightly around the rail three times and brought back and over the rear rail. The pair of strands are now tightly wrapped two times over the rear rail and brought up on the inside of the rail. Here, several ½-inch #20 brads are used to nail the sea grass to the chair rail. Note that the nails do not carry the weight of the chair's occupant. The nails merely keep the grass from unwinding. The turns lock the grass in place. Now the ends of the grass strands are cut flush with the top of the rear rail. If you have too much sea grass left over, cut the following pieces a little shorter.

At this juncture, you have six turns of sea grass on the front rail adjoining its right end, let us say. Then you have a pair of strands going straight back to the end of the rear chair rail. The pair of strands make two complete turns and are nailed in place.

The second pair of warp strands are now installed the same way. Again, the start of the pair is held in place by the turns; in the case of the second and subsequent warp pairs, however, there are only two complete turns because you just want 1 inch of spacing. The end of the second pair of warp strands is wrapped around the rear rail for two complete turns and nailed, again to make a space of 1 inch.

This sequence is repeated until all the warp strands are in place. If the pattern doesn't work out evenly, add a few spacing turns or remove a few turns, or push them apart a little. A slight unevenness will never be noticed.

The first warp is started at the end of the front chair rail. The pencil mark is in line with the end of the rear chair rail. The folded end of the grass is held in place by the turns. When the pair of strands in the craftsman's hand is brought down and back, the side of the second strand will be on the pencil mark.

The first warp has been brought back to the end of the rear rail and wrapped around the rear rail. The two strand ends have been nailed in place.

The warp on the front chair rail is being finished up. If you look closely, you will see that the plan failed; a couple of extra filler turns are needed on the left end of the front rail. But note that all the warp strands run straight back and are parallel to each other.

More pairs of warp strands have been positioned. The ends of the third strand pair are being nailed to the rear chair rail. Note the spacing between strands.

Installing the woof strands
The woof strands are started at the front left or front right of the chair. The first strand, a single strand of sea grass, is nailed to the inside or bottom of the side bar. Then the strand is wrapped once or twice around the side bar and carried across the warp strands; going under one, over the next, and so on. It doesn't matter if you start out going under the first pair of warp strands or over. What matters is that you maintain the pattern. Changes here are easily spotted.

When you come to the other side bar, the woof strand is brought over and around for one full turn so that there is always one turn alongside each woof strand.

Since you began with one or two turns and then crossed over, you will have to wrap one or two "filler" turns around the front end of the side rail to make the woof strands run straight across.

You can use a double woof strand if you wish; you can use more spacing turns between woof strands if you wish. It is all a matter of choice. The seat bottom will be lots stronger than the chair itself no matter what pattern you select.

In any case, continue with the woofing until you come to the end of the particular piece of grass you are using. Then, either nail the end to the inside or underside of the rail and start the succeeding length of grass on another nail or knot the two pieces together and keep on woofing. If you position the knot carefully it will rest on the inside of the frame and will be almost invisible.

As you woof, press the strands toward the front of the chair to help keep them in line with the turns of sea grass over the side rails.

When you are within an inch or so of the rear rail, you will find it very, very difficult to continue the weaving process. So just cover one side rail's end with turns and nail the end of the grass strand in place. Then wrap some filler turns around the remaining bare section on the other side rail.

That finishes the seat bottom. Nothing more need be done to it.

Now the woof has been started. It is under, over, and so on; then there is a full turn around the side rail to provide one turn of spacing between adjoining woof strands.

The woofing continues. Here is the technique used. The sea grass is folded to make it easier to pass it between the warp strands. As each woof strand is positioned, it is pushed back alongside its fellows so that the center of the strand is always in line with its ends. Incidentally, the best place to sit while doing this is on a small box in front of the chair.

The completed rewoven chair bottom. There are a couple of errors. Can you spot them?

APPENDIX: SOURCES OF SUPPLY

The following companies handle mail order as well as accept personal caller orders. Some issue catalogues. All postal applications should be made directly to the company concerned accompanied by a stamped addressed envelope.

RATTAN CANE
Sold as diameter sizes in pole lengths or bundles:

Jacobs, Young & Westbury Ltd.,
J.Y.W. House,
Bridge Road,
Haywards Heath,
Sussex.
Tel: Haywards Heath (0444) 412411

The Cane Store,
377 Seven Sisters Road,
London, N.15.
Tel: 01-802 8195

Berkhamsted Arts & Crafts,
3 London Road,
Berkhamsted,
Herts.
Tel: Berkhamstead (04427) 6632

Deben Craftsmen,
9 St. Peter Street,
Ipswich,
Suffolk.
Tel: Ipswich (0473) 215042

Dunlicraft Ltd.,
Pullman Road,
Wigston,
Leicester LE8 2DY
Tel: Leicester (0533) 811040

Berry's Craft Supplies,
10 Hill Road,
Theydon Bois,
Epping,
Essex.
Tel: Theydon Bois (037881) 3532

Dryad Ltd.,
P.O. Box 38,
Northgates,
Leicester, LE1 9BU
Tel: Leicester (0533) 50405

Companies selling related products are shown below and an asterisk to the left of the name indicates that the address is given above:

CANE WEBBING (sometimes called sheet cane)

Machine and hand woven cane for seating and backing chairs, screen panels etc. Available in a variety of patterns and weaves and in various widths.
Sold by the square foot, or by length.

* Jacobs, Young & Westbury Ltd.
* The Cane Store.
* Berkhamsted Arts & Crafts.
* Deben Craftsmen.
* Berry's Craft Supplies.
* Dryad Ltd.

REED/CENTRE CANE

The term *Reed* as used in page 9 and elswhere in the book, is known throughout the U.K. as *Centre Cane* and is used for some decorative work on furniture as well as in basketry work.
Sold in a variety of sizes by weight.

* Jacobs, Young & Westbury Ltd.
* The Cane Store.
* Berkhamsted Arts & Crafts.
* Deben Craftsmen.
* Dunlicraft Ltd.
* Berry's Cane Supplies.
* Dryad Ltd.

Fred Aldous Ltd.,
P.O. Box 135,
37 Lever Street,
Manchester M60 1UX
Tel: 061-236 2477

Smit & Co. Ltd.,
99 Walnut Tree Close,
Guildford, Surrey,
GM1 4UQ
Tel: 0483 33113

SPLINT/FLAT BAND

The term *splint* as used in pages 12/13 and elsewhere in the book is known in the UK as *flat band*.
It is sold by weight.

* Jacobs, Young & Westbury Ltd.
* The Cane Store.
* Deben Craftsmen.
* Dryad Ltd.
* Berry's Craft Supplies.
* Smit & Co., Ltd.

STRAND CANE

This is commonly known as *chair cane* or *lapping cane* and is used for binding canes together or for weaving chair seats and backs etc.
Sold in hanks by weight.

* Jacobs, Young & Westbury Ltd.
* The Cane Store.
* Berkhamsted Arts & Crafts.
* Deben Craftsmen.
* Dunlicraft Ltd.
* Berry's Craft Supplies.
* Dryad Ltd.
* Smit & Co. Ltd.

SEA GRASS
For Seat weaving.
Sold in hanks or bales by weight.

* Jacobs, Young & Westbury Ltd.
* The Cane Store.
* Berkhamsted Arts & Crafts.
* Deben Craftsmen.
* Dunlicraft.
* Berry's Craft Supplies.
* Dryad Ltd.
* Fred Aldous.
* Smit & Co. Ltd.

RUSH & FIBRE RUSH
Rush is the natural plant found in rivers and is the traditional material used in seating. It is sold by the bolt.
Fibre Rush (artificial rush) is a manufactured product made mainly from twisted paper. It is sold in coils or bundles by weight.

Suppliers are indicated thus: Rush † Fibre Rush ‡

* Jacobs, Young & Westbury Ltd. † ‡
* The Cane Store. †
* Berkhamsted Arts & Crafts. † ‡
* Deben Craftsmen. †
* Berry's Craft Supplies. † ‡
* Dryad Ltd. †
I. & J. L. Brown, †
58 Commercial Road,
Hereford, HR1 2BP.
Tel: Hereford (0432) 58895

In addition to the foregoing companies, cane, sea grass and rush suppliers may be found in large town or city craft shops that cover a wide range of subjects and materials. Other mail order companies advertise in local papers or directories e.g. Yellow Pages.

CANEWORKER'S TOOLS
Mainly seating and backing weaving tools.

* Jacobs, Young & Westbury Ltd.
* Berry's Craft Supplies.
* Dryad Ltd.
* Berkhamsted Arts & Crafts.
* The Cane Store.
* Smit & Co. Ltd.

PROPANE TORCHES

Some torches are supplied as torch, hose and connector and made to fit standard connections of domestic cylinders of propane or butane gas (e.g. Calor Gas); others as torches complete with cannister of gas.

Flamefast Ltd.,
Pendlebury Industrial Estate,
Bridge Street,
Swindon,
Manchester M27 1FJ.
Tel: 061-793 9333
(Sell 'T4' General Purpose Torch).

Griffin & George Ltd.,
285 Ealing Road,
Wembley,
Middx. HA0 1HJ.
Tel: 01-997 3344.
(Sell 'Flamemaster Torch').

* Dryad Ltd.
  (Sell 'Taymar' all purpose torch complete with gas).

Other D.I.Y. stores, such as branches of Robert Dyas Ltd., sell this and/or similar products made by, amongst others, Ronson Ltd.

Cylinders of domestic gas are available from hardware stores, camping and caravanning stores and some general builders' merchants.

INDEX

Alcohol, 194
Angle joints, 32
    defined, 29
    maximum strength, 32
    wrapping, 45
Arch brace, 93, 136, 159, 175,
    178, 179, 185
    bending, 92
    long, 113-114
    ornamental, 130
    short, 115
Armrests, 163
Arms, 177-178
Ash, 14
Ash splint chart, 13
Assembly, trial, 73-74

Back leg braces, 179
Back legs, 167
Backrest, 162
    central support, 164
    fastening top bar, 163, 164
    installing slats, 164-165
    middle support, 164
    support, 162, 163
Backrest cushion, 166
Bamboo, 3
Basic frame, 155-156, 157
Bed bench, 105-118
    designs for, 67
    partial assembly, 111
    parts list, 105
    variations, 106
Bending, 73
    cold, 22-23
    cold, wet, 23-24
    hot, 24, 26
Bends, curls, and curves, 69
Binding cane, 165
Bleaching, 63
    effects of, 63
Brace(s), 112
    arch, 92, 136, 359, 175, 178,
    179, 185
    right-angle, 116, 126, 129, 151,
    157-158
    straight, 90-91
    temporary, 115
Broken joints, 197
Brush, 61, 189
Burlap, 120, 121, 126, 128,
    181

finishing, 130
steam-pressed, 122
trimming, 128, 129
varnished, 144

Cane
    finishing, 62
    for ornamentation, 47
    wrapping, 38-40
    wrappings that hide, 49
Cane length, formula for, 39
Cane webbed seat, replacing,
    198-201
Cane webbing, 120, 124, 181, 186
    closely woven, 187
    cutting, 108
    dimensions of, 7
    sealing, 117, 189
    styles of, 8
    tightly woven, 107
    well-soaked, 200
Care, 62
Casters, 143, 144
    installing, 146
Central backrest support, 154
Chair(s)
    back, 171
    designs for, 66
    frame, 172-173
    seats, 64, 194-195
Chaise longue, 132-142
    designs for, 67, 133
    parts list, 132
Chalk-string-nail compass, 90
Chamfer, 83, 138, 144, 146, 152,
    155, 160, 173, 174
Checkers table. See Night table
Chipboard, 107, 120, 121, 124,
    144, 182, 186, 187, 188
Circles
    adjoining, 51, 59
    continuous, 52, 59
    diminishing-diameter, 53
    independent, 50, 57
Clamp(s), 112, 178. 187
    C, 18
    spring, 18
Cleaning, 63
Clefs, 57
Clear enamel, 142, 165
Clear sealer, 189
Cleats, 157, 183

Climbing palm, 3
Clothes tree, 97-104
  assembly, 102
  bending bars, 99-100
  center pole, 98
  finishing, 104
  leveling, 104
  making holes, 99
  parts list, 97
Coffee table, 81-86, 87-96
  accuracy, 84-85
  assembly, 84, 85
  bending and erecting arms,
    89-90
  designs for, 66
  height, 81
  hoops, 81, 84
  legs for, 83
  main arms, 88
  parts list, 81, 87
  variations, 88
Components, building to, 68
Concave curve, 30
Construction tips, 72-77
Corner joints, 35
  defined, 29
  wrapping, 45-46
Corners, trimming, 108
Couch. See Love seat
Countersinking, 31, 33, 38, 109,
    114, 127, 146, 149, 155,
    177, 184
Crisscross braces, 174, 175
Crossbars
  installing, 102, 130, 139-140
  making, 99
  top, 167
Cross braces, 160, 161
Curls (spirals), 55
Curved end pieces, 163
Cushions, 154, 155
Cutting
  guides, 21
  measuring, 21
  plan, 72-73
Cutting and bending, 19-28

Denatured alcohol, 62
Design, defined, 64
Designing, 70-71
  freehand sketch, 70
  making a model, 71
  scale of drawing, 71
Detergent, 23

Diameter, 5
Dimensions, basic, 65
Dining room chairs, 166-179
  assembling, 169-172
  basic design, 166-167
  parts list, 166
Double-weight window glass, 143
Drawings, full size, 73
Dressing-table seat, 106
Drill, electric, 18
Duco cement, 31, 39, 42, 50,
    116, 197
Duck feet, 181

Edge screws, 107
Ends, sealing, 117
Elmer's glue, 42, 107, 187, 200
Enamel, 86, 179, 189
  clear, 142, 165
Equipment, for working with
    rattan, 17
Étagére, 119-131, 181
  assembly, 124-130
  designs, 119, 120-121
  materials, 120
  parts list, 119

Fading, 193
Fiber rush, 14
  colors of, 14
Fiber (reed) splint chart, 13
File, 86, 181, 188
Flat reed, 13
Flat/oval reed chart, 10
Flat reed chart, 10
Flower stand. See Night table
Flowers, 56-57
Finish
  applying, 61
  choice of, 60
  clear, 60
Finishing and care, 60-63
  preparation for, 61
Folded (or bent) joint, 34-35
  defined, 29
  wrapping, 45
Foot rest, 106
Frame members, 134
Frame sides, 134-136
  assembling, 136
  bracing, 138
  joining, 138-139
Freehand sketch of bend, 19
Front legs, 167

Front rail spacing, 203
Furniture polish, 63
Furring strips, 83

Glass, positioning, 94
Glass-top table, 87
Grindstone, 100, 109, 169
Groove(s), 83, 199
Guardbar (rail), 150
Guard rails, making, 151
Guide(s), 145, 149, 157
   scrap lumber, 73
Guide blocks, 136
Guide board, 181

Hacksaw, 19
Handle(s), 149
   attaching, 116
   wrapping, 116
Hardwood splint, 14
Hole-to-leg end dimension, 168
Hong Kong grass. *See* Sea grass
Hooks
   fastening, 104
   making, 101-102
Hoops, 81, 84
Horseshoe braces, 149-150

Jig(s), 74-75, 83, 114
   making, 99
Joints, 29-46
   angle, 32
   corner, 35
   folded, or bent, 34-35
   handle-to-leg, 117
   mortise-and-tenon, 36
   parallel, 36
   pinned, 37-38
   splices, 33
   T, 30
   types of, 29
   wrapping, 38-39, 92, 102, 165

Knots, 107
Knots and glue method, 42
Knots and nails method, 42
Knotted wrapping, 41

Lacquer, 60, 86, 161
   clear, 179
   flat, 60
   gloss, 60
   quick-drying, 193
Lamp stand. *See* Night table

Layout board, 17
Leg "feet," 183
Legs, 111, 144-146, 156, 181
   bending, 100-101, 110
   cutting and marking, 145, 159
   fastening, 103
   finishing, 101
   making, 100
Loading, defined, 69
Lollipops, 56
Love seat, 153-165
   designs for, 67
   parts list, 153
   variations, 154

Machine cane. *See* Cane webbing
Masking tape, 45, 51, 73, 92, 178
Materials, 3-14
Maximum angle-joint strength, 32
Memory, defined, 22
Mild bleach, 63
Miter box, 19
Model, building a, 64-65
Moisture, 63
Mortise(s), 111, 169, 170, 171,
     172, 173, 183, 184
Mortise-and-tenon joints, 36-37,
     183
   defined, 29

Nail joint, 31
New rattan, finishing, 60
Night table, 180-189
   assembly, 182-183
   designs for, 66
   parts list, 180
   variations, 181

Ocher, 43, 102, 131, 142, 189
Old rattan, finishing, 62
Ornamentation, 47-59
   broken, 198
Overbending, 22, 23

Paint, 60
   on rattan, damaged, 193-194
   removal, 63, 194
   on wicker, damaged, 194
Paint colors, matching, 193
Painted wicker, very old, 197
Paint remover, 62, 194
Parallel joint(s), 36
   defined, 29

Pattern
    making a, 99
    setting up a, 85-86
Pegged method, 43
Pilot drill, 31
Pilot hole(s), 93, 103, 109, 112,
        148, 156, 186
Pinned joint, 30, 37-38
Plane, small, 18
Plywood, 107
Pole diameters, 76-77
Pole end(s)
    binding, 47
    treating, 47
Pole length, 69
Poles, cutting, 122
Polyurethane
    gloss, 61
    matt, 61
Power grinder, 182
Powered sprayer, 61
Precision, 75
Propane torch, 16, 17, 25
Putty, 38, 77, 102, 131, 142
    colored, 117, 149, 152, 161,
        165, 179, 189

Rabbets, 123, 124
Rails, supporting, 202
Rain, effect of, 86
Rattan
    bending, 22
    definition of, 3
    dimensions of, 4
    grading of, 4
    measuring to cut, 21
    ornamentation, 57
    species and quality of, 4
    split, 59
Rattan furniture
    designing, 64-71
    storage of, 62
    supporting surfaces, 68
Rattan holder, 19
Razor knife, 43, 50, 108, 126, 128,
        169, 179, 182, 187, 201
Reed, 3, 9, 50
    chart, 10
    dimensions of, 9
    finishing, 62
    handicraft, 9
    waves, 54
Reed splint, 13, 175
Repainting, 193-194

Repairs, 191-206
Reweaving a chair, 201-202
Ridges, paint surface, 193
Right-angle support, 168
Round bulk reed chart, 12
Router, electric, 18
Rungs, 167

Sandpaper, 86, 130, 142, 165, 179,
        186, 188
    to clean grooves, 199
    in repairing rattan, 193
Scant stock, 99
Scrap wood guide, 147
Scraped rattan. See Skinned
        rattan
Screw joint, 31
Sea grass, 14, 63, 201, 202, 203,
        205, 206
Seal, 152, 179, 189
Seat, 107, 156
    ends of, 112
    sides, 108
Seat and back, weaving, 175-177
Seat frame, 167, 169, 170, 173,
        174
    rear bar, 171
Seat splint, 176, 177
Semicircle, ornamentation, 54
Settee. See Love seat
Shelf(ves), 183
    completing, 187-188
    cutting and fastening, 184
    making, 121
    sides, 186
    support bars, 184, 185
Shelf frames, 146
Shellac, 62
    orange, 121
    white, 121
Side bars, 173
Silicon, 19, 60, 142, 165, 169
    effect on knives, 182
Skinned rattan, 8
    qualities of, 8
    use of varnish on, 8
    working with, 28
Smoothly skinned rattan, 8-9
Sofa. See Love seat
Sources of supply, 207-208
Spaced wrappings, 48
Spiral wrappings, 49
Splice(s), 33, 45, 86
    defined, 29

Spline, 7, 199-201
Spline chart, 11
Splint, 3, 12-14
    finishing, 62
Split rattan, 59, 186, 187, 188
Spot painting, 193
Spray cans, 61, 193, 194
    distance between can and work
        piece, 61
Spray gun, 194
Stapler, 175
Staples, 175, 176
Stock, separating, 72
Straight back chair, 178-179
Straight braces, 90-91, 158, 159,
        178
    installing, 140
Strand cane, 6
    dimensions of, 6, 7
Stretchers. *See* Rungs
Stripping, 63, 194
        See also Paint removal
Supporting bars, 202
Surform file, 83
Surform plane, 96, 109, 181,
        184, 185
Surform round file, 18

T joint, 30
    defined, 29
    shaping butted end, 30
    wrapping, 44
Tables, designs for, 66
Tabletop(s), 64, 65, 182
    completing, 187
    glass, 81, 88, 90
Tea cart, 143-152
    assembling, 147-148
    design variations, 144
    parts list, 143
Telephone stand. *See* Night table
Temperature, 61
Tenon(s), 109, 111, 169, 171, 174
Thick poles, hot bending
    bending, 25
    burns and other damage, 27
    controlling bend, 25
    cooling, 25
    correcting bend, 27
    setup for, 25
Thin poles
    native technique, 28
    setup for, 27
Tools
    special, 18

    for working with cane, reed, 17
    for working with rattan, 15
Tools and equipment, 15-18
"Tooth," defined, 61
Torch
    gasoline, 16
    propane, 16, 17, 25
    spreading nozzle, 16
Torch flame, 181
Trim, 116, 126
Try square, 114
Two-solution bleach, 63

U bolts, 16, 19
Utility bench, 106
Utility table. *See* Night table

Varnish, 86, 106, 107, 142, 179
    clear, 161, 189
Vermeer, 193
Verticalness, 85
Vise, 15

Warp, 202, 203
    first, 204
    installing strands, 203-204
Waves, 54-55, 59
Wax, 63
Webbed cane, 144
Weight. *See* Loading
"Wet" coating, 61
Wicker
    artificial, 3
    stripping, 194
Wicker armrests and backs
    loose, 196
    refastening, 196
Wicker furniture, 3
Wicker seats
    loose, 194
    refastening, 195
Wide binding cane, 6
Willow, 3
Wood bleach, commercial, 63
Wood guide, 20
Wood splint, 13
    dimensions of, 14
    qualities of, 13
Woof, 222
    installing strands, 205-206
Workbench, 16
Woven splint, 179
Wrapping, 38-40, 85-86
    cane length, 38-39